PERFORMANCE SUMMARY:

(amounts in billions, except for diluted earnings per share and store count)	Fiscal 2006	Fiscal 2005	Fiscal 2004
Net sales	$ 90.8	$ 81.5	$ 73.1
Net earnings	$ 5.8	$ 5.8	$ 5.0
Diluted earnings per share	$ 2.79	$ 2.72	$ 2.26
Total assets	$ 52.3	$ 44.4	$ 39.0
Total liabilities	$ 27.2	$ 17.5	$ 14.9
Stockholders' equity	$ 25.0	$ 26.9	$ 24.2
Store count	2,147	2,042	1,890

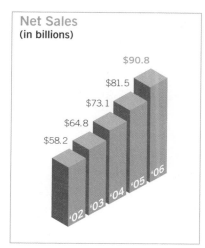

Net Sales
(in billions)

$58.2 '02
$64.8 '03
$73.1 '04
$81.5 '05
$90.8 '06

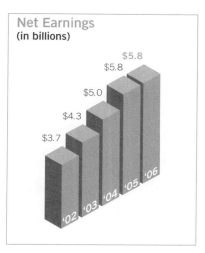

Net Earnings
(in billions)

$3.7 '02
$4.3 '03
$5.0 '04
$5.8 '05
$5.8 '06

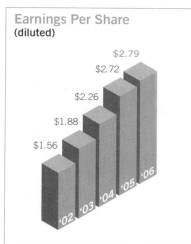

Earnings Per Share
(diluted)

$1.56 '02
$1.88 '03
$2.26 '04
$2.72 '05
$2.79 '06

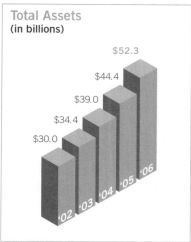

Total Assets
(in billions)

$30.0 '02
$34.4 '03
$39.0 '04
$44.4 '05
$52.3 '06

DEAR SHAREHOLDERS, ASSOCIATES, CUSTOMERS, SUPPLIERS AND COMMUNITIES:

From the beginning, outstanding customer service has been the cornerstone of our company. Our customers have high expectations of us because our associates set them. This expectation of outstanding customer service is what sets us apart as a retailer. The most critical job for those of us leading this company is to sustain a culture that never falls short of those customer expectations. Our "values wheel" summarizes that culture:

As you'll read in the attached financial report, 2006 was a challenging year for us. We experienced a tough housing market, particularly in the second half of the year. We addressed this challenge by accelerating investment in our retail business and intensifying our focus on customer service and satisfaction.

Going forward, we expect 2007 to be a challenging year as the housing environment remains soft. We will continue to make the necessary investments in our retail business so that we will emerge even stronger when the industry recovers. We are focused on five priorities around which our leadership team, our associates and our investments are aligned.

Associate engagement: Deliver differentiated customer service and the know-how our customers have come to expect from The Home Depot.

Product excitement: Drive value, price leadership and innovation through merchandising.

Product availability: Improve in-stock positions so customers can find and buy exactly what they need.

Shopping environment: Ensure that our stores are safe, clean and uncluttered.

Own the Pro: Be the number one destination for professional contractors, whose business today makes up roughly 30 percent of our retail sales.

2006 was a milestone year for our Supply segment. We completed the acquisition of Hughes Supply and successfully integrated it into our HD Supply business. We are now the second largest commercial distribution business in the United States. As we announced in February 2007, we are exploring strategic alternatives for HD Supply, including a possible sale of the business.

In 2006, we made a significant acquisition in China, a country with one of the largest and fastest growing home improvement markets in the world. The company we acquired, The Home Way, has stores that look very similar to ours in North America for a very good reason: We trained its founding management team in the mid 1990s.

Our goal is to provide the best customer experience in home improvement retail, the best place to work for our associates and the best place to invest. The five priorities described above are clearly aligned with the first two goals, and we will use a disciplined capital allocation approach to drive toward the third goal.

The most important barometer of the health of our company is the health of our culture. I hope that you shop our stores and experience our customer-focused culture firsthand.

Frank

Francis S. Blake
Chairman & Chief Executive Officer
March 29, 2007

OUR ASSOCIATES MAKE THE DIFFERENCE.

At The Home Depot, we believe in taking care of the people who take care of our customers. Our 364,000 associates have the know-how and the desire to make a real difference to the customer experience. We invest in our associates because they are our most important asset. We offer our associates extensive training programs, Success Sharing and Orange Juiced rewards and bonuses, as well as industry-leading benefits for full- and part-time associates. Taking care of our people is one of our core values – it's part of our culture.

SERVING CUSTOMERS

EVER SINCE WE OPENED OUR FIRST STORE, OUR FOCUS HAS BEEN ON PROVIDING OUR CUSTOMERS WITH OUTSTANDING CUSTOMER SERVICE, AS WELL AS CONVENIENCE, VALUE, QUALITY AND PRODUCT AND PROJECT KNOW-HOW.

In 2006, we continued to improve our customer shopping experience by upgrading the appearance of many of our stores. We also served our customers by providing innovative products, from tools and hardware to lighting and outdoor living – all at great values. Our business is delivering service and doing it in a way that makes our associates and customers proud.

WHATEVER THE NEED - LARGE OR SMALL, SIMPLE OR COMPLEX - WE KNOW THAT CUSTOMERS DEPEND ON THE HOME DEPOT TO DELIVER VALUE.

We know that value means different things to different customers. Our professional customers want to be able to quickly find the right product, in the right quantity, at an everyday low price. We create value for them by increasing the productivity of their business. Do-it-yourself (DIY) customers need a great selection of quality name brand merchandise at a great price, and they need knowledgeable associates to help them select everything they need to complete their project. We create value for our DIY customers by helping them achieve their home improvement dreams.

Visit us online at www.homedepot.com

BUILDING COMMUNITIES

BUILDING COMMUNITIES IS AT THE HEART OF OUR COMPANY'S CULTURE.
OUR ASSOCIATES USE THEIR TALENT AND PASSION TO MAKE A DIFFERENCE.

When disaster strikes a community, The Home Depot and its associates are the first to step forward with response and recovery efforts. In 2006, we were the lead contributor of Hands On Network's Corporate Month of Service. Working with our partners, such as KaBOOM! and the American Red Cross, we touched more than 1,000 communities with 1,000 partners and 40,000 volunteers across North America, including the hurricane-ravaged Gulf Coast. We helped dig, plant and construct - not just foundations, trees and affordable housing - but the groundwork, memories and bonds that will last a lifetime.

Learn more about The Home Depot's community involvement at www.homedepot.com/corporateresponsibility

UNITED STATES
SECURITIES AND EXCHANGE COMMISSION
WASHINGTON, D.C. 20549

FORM 10-K

☒ **ANNUAL REPORT PURSUANT TO SECTION 13 OR 15(d) OF THE SECURITIES EXCHANGE ACT OF 1934**

For the fiscal year ended January 28, 2007

OR

☐ **TRANSITION REPORT PURSUANT TO SECTION 13 OR 15(d) OF THE SECURITIES EXCHANGE ACT OF 1934**

Commission File Number 1-8207

THE HOME DEPOT, INC.
(Exact Name of Registrant as Specified in its Charter)

DELAWARE
(State or Other Jurisdiction of Incorporation or Organization)

95-3261426
(I.R.S. Employer Identification No.)

2455 PACES FERRY ROAD, N.W., ATLANTA, GEORGIA 30339
(Address of Principal Executive Offices) (Zip Code)

Registrant's Telephone Number, Including Area Code: **(770) 433-8211**

SECURITIES REGISTERED PURSUANT TO SECTION 12(b) OF THE ACT:

TITLE OF EACH CLASS	NAME OF EACH EXCHANGE ON WHICH REGISTERED
Common Stock, $0.05 Par Value Per Share	New York Stock Exchange

SECURITIES REGISTERED PURSUANT TO SECTION 12(g) OF THE ACT: **None**

Indicate by check mark if the Registrant is a well-known seasoned issuer, as defined in Rule 405 of the Securities Act. Yes ☒ No ☐

Indicate by check mark if the Registrant is not required to file reports pursuant to Section 13 or Section 15(d) of the Act. Yes ☐ No ☒

Indicate by check mark whether the Registrant (1) has filed all reports required to be filed by Section 13 or 15(d) of the Securities Exchange Act of 1934 during the preceding 12 months (or for such shorter period that the Registrant was required to file such reports), and (2) has been subject to such filing requirements for the past 90 days. Yes ☒ No ☐

Indicate by check mark if disclosure of delinquent filers pursuant to Item 405 of Regulation S-K is not contained herein, and will not be contained, to the best of Registrant's knowledge, in definitive proxy or information statements incorporated by reference in Part III of this Form 10-K or any amendment to this Form 10-K. ☐

Indicate by check mark whether the Registrant is a large accelerated filer, an accelerated filer, or a non-accelerated filer. See definition of "accelerated filer and large accelerated filer" in Rule 12b-2 of the Exchange Act.

Large accelerated filer ☒   Accelerated filer ☐   Non-accelerated filer ☐

Indicate by check mark whether the Registrant is a shell company (as defined in Rule 12b-2 of the Exchange Act). Yes ☐ No ☒

The aggregate market value of the Common Stock of the Registrant held by non-affiliates of the Registrant on July 30, 2006 was $70.6 billion.

The number of shares outstanding of the Registrant's Common Stock as of March 26, 2007 was 1,969,535,236 shares.

DOCUMENTS INCORPORATED BY REFERENCE

Portions of the Registrant's proxy statement for the 2007 Annual Meeting of Shareholders are incorporated by reference in Part III of this Form 10-K to the extent described herein.

THE HOME DEPOT, INC.
FISCAL YEAR 2006 FORM 10-K

TABLE OF CONTENTS

CAUTIONARY STATEMENT PURSUANT TO THE
PRIVATE SECURITIES LITIGATION REFORM ACT OF 1995

Certain statements regarding our future performance made in this report are forward-looking statements. Forward-looking statements may relate to such matters as Net Sales growth, comparable store sales, impact of cannibalization, state of the residential construction and housing markets, commodity price inflation and deflation, implementation of store initiatives, protection of intellectual property rights, Net Earnings performance, including Depreciation and Amortization expense, earnings per share, stock-based compensation expense, store openings and closures, capital allocation and expenditures, the effect of adopting certain accounting standards, return on invested capital, management of our purchasing or customer credit policies, strategic direction, including whether or not a sale or initial public offering of HD Supply will occur or, if a transaction is undertaken, its terms or timing, and the demand for our products and services.

These statements are based on currently available information and our current assumptions, expectations and projections about future events. While we believe that our assumptions, expectations and projections are reasonable in view of the currently available information, you are cautioned not to place undue reliance on our forward-looking statements. These statements are not guarantees of future performance. They are subject to future events, risks and uncertainties – many of which are beyond our control – as well as potentially inaccurate assumptions, that could cause actual results to differ materially from our expectations and projections. Some of the material risks and uncertainties that could cause actual results to differ materially from our expectations and projections are described in Item 1A. "Risk Factors." You should read that information in conjunction with "Management's Discussion and Analysis of Financial Condition and Results of Operations" in Item 7 of this report and our Consolidated Financial Statements and related notes in Item 8 of this report. We note such information for investors as permitted by the Private Securities Litigation Reform Act of 1995. There also may be other factors that we cannot anticipate or that are not described in this report, generally because we do not perceive them to be material, that could cause results to differ materially from our expectations.

Forward-looking statements speak only as of the date they are made, and we do not undertake to update these forward-looking statements. You are advised, however, to review any further disclosures we make on related subjects in our periodic filings with the Securities and Exchange Commission ("SEC").

PART I

Item 1. Business.

Introduction

The Home Depot, Inc. is the world's largest home improvement retailer and the second largest retailer in the United States ("U.S."), based on Net Sales for the fiscal year ended January 28, 2007 ("fiscal 2006"). As of the end of fiscal 2006, we were operating 2,147 stores, most of which are The Home Depot stores.

The Home Depot stores sell a wide assortment of building materials, home improvement and lawn and garden products and provide a number of services. The Home Depot stores average approximately 105,000 square feet of enclosed space, with approximately 23,000 additional square feet of outside garden area. As of the end of fiscal 2006, we had 2,100 The Home Depot stores located throughout the U.S. (including the territories of Puerto Rico and the Virgin Islands), Canada, China and Mexico. In addition, at the end of fiscal 2006, the Company operated 34 EXPO Design Center stores, 11 The Home Depot Landscape Supply stores and two The Home Depot Floor stores.

In addition to our retail stores, our business includes HD Supply, which distributes products and sells installation services primarily to business-to-business customers, including home builders, professional contractors, municipalities and maintenance professionals. HD Supply consists of four major platforms: 1) infrastructure, including waterworks and utilities; 2) construction, including construction supply, lumber and building materials, electrical, plumbing/HVAC and interiors; 3) maintenance, including facilities maintenance and industrial PVF; and 4) repair and remodel.

In February 2007, the Company announced its decision to evaluate strategic alternatives for HD Supply, including a possible sale or initial public offering of the business. There can be no assurance that any transaction will occur or, if one is undertaken, its terms or timing.

The Home Depot, Inc. is a Delaware corporation that was incorporated in 1978. Our Store Support Center (corporate office) is located at 2455 Paces Ferry Road, N.W., Atlanta, Georgia 30339. Our telephone number is (770) 433-8211.

We maintain an Internet website at www.homedepot.com. We make available on our website, free of charge, our Annual Reports to shareholders, Annual Reports on Form 10-K, Quarterly Reports on Form 10-Q, Current Reports on Form 8-K, Proxy Statements and Forms 3, 4 and 5 as soon as reasonably practicable after filing such documents with, or furnishing such documents to, the SEC.

We include our website addresses throughout this filing only as textual references. The information contained on our websites is not incorporated by reference into this Form 10-K.

Our Business

We operate in two reportable segments, Retail and HD Supply. You will find information concerning the financial results and the total assets of each segment in Note 12 to the Consolidated Financial Statements. Financial information about our operations outside the United States is also reported in Note 12 to the Consolidated Financial Statements.

Retail Segment

Operating Strategy. Our operating strategy is to offer a broad assortment of high-quality merchandise and services at competitive prices using knowledgeable, service-oriented personnel and strong marketing and credit promotions. We believe that our associates' knowledge of products and home improvement techniques and applications is very important to our marketing approach and our ability to maintain and enhance customer satisfaction.

Customers. The Home Depot stores serve three primary customer groups:

- **Do-It-Yourself ("D-I-Y") Customers:** These customers are typically home owners who purchase products and complete their own projects and installations. To complement the expertise of our associates, The Home Depot stores offer "how-to" clinics taught by associates and merchandise vendors.

- **Do-It-For-Me ("D-I-F-M") Customers:** These customers are typically home owners who purchase materials themselves and hire third parties to complete the project and/or installation. We arrange for the installation of a variety of The Home Depot products through qualified independent contractors.

- **Professional Customers:** These customers are professional remodelers, general contractors, repairmen and tradesmen. In many stores, we offer a variety of programs to these customers, including additional delivery and will-call services, dedicated staff, extensive merchandise selections and expanded credit programs, all of which we believe increase sales to these customers.

Products. A typical The Home Depot store stocks 35,000 to 45,000 products during the year, including both national brand name and proprietary items. The following table shows the percentage of Net Sales of each major product group (and related services) for each of the last three fiscal years:

Product Group	Percentage of Net Sales for Fiscal Year Ended		
	January 28, 2007	January 29, 2006	January 30, 2005
Building materials, lumber and millwork	**23.6%**	24.2%	24.4%
Plumbing, electrical and kitchen	**30.8**	29.4	29.0
Hardware and seasonal	**27.0**	27.1	26.9
Paint, flooring and wall covering	**18.6**	19.3	19.7
Total	**100.0%**	100.0%	100.0%

To complement and enhance our product selection, we have formed strategic alliances and exclusive relationships with selected suppliers to market products under a variety of well-recognized brand names. During fiscal 2006, we offered a number of proprietary and exclusive brands across a wide range of departments including, but not limited to, Behr Premium Plus® paint, Charmglow® gas grills, Hampton Bay® lighting, Mills Pride® cabinets, Vigoro® lawn care products, Husky® hand tools, RIDGID® and Ryobi® power tools, Pegasus® faucets, Traffic Master® carpet, Glacier Bay® bath fixtures and Veranda® decking products. We may consider additional strategic alliances and relationships with other suppliers and will continue to assess opportunities to expand the range of products available under brand names that are exclusive to The Home Depot.

In fiscal 2006, innovative and distinctive products continued to be a growth driver supporting our merchandising strategy. The following successes helped differentiate The Home Depot in the marketplace:

- Introduced the most comprehensive lineup of top brand lawn tractors and mowers available nationwide, including Cub Cadet®, Toro®, John Deere® and Honda®;

- Launched an expanded outdoor living assortment, including Hampton Bay patio and Charmglow grills;

- Launched an exclusive line-up of lithium-ion power tools from Milwaukee®, RIDGID and Makita®; and

- Launched the LG® SteamWasher™ and the Maytag® Epic™ washer and dryer.

We maintain a global sourcing merchandise program to source high-quality products directly from manufacturers. Our product development merchants travel internationally to identify opportunities to purchase items directly for our stores. Additionally, we have four sourcing offices located in Shanghai, Shenzhen, Dalian, and Chengdu, China, as well as one office in Gurgaon, India. We also have a quality assurance engineer located in Milan, Italy and we have product development merchants, as well as a sourcing office, in Monterrey, Mexico. We currently source products from more than 800 factories in approximately 35 countries.

Services. The Home Depot and EXPO Design Center stores offer a variety of installation services. These services target D-I-F-M customers who select and purchase products and installation of those products from us. These installation programs include products such as carpeting, flooring, cabinets, countertops and water heaters. In addition, we provide professional installation of a number of products sold through our in-home sales programs, such as generators and furnace and central air systems.

Store Growth

United States.   At the end of fiscal 2006, we were operating 1,872 The Home Depot stores in the U.S., including the territories of Puerto Rico and the Virgin Islands. During fiscal 2006, we opened 86 new The Home Depot stores, including eight relocations, in the U.S.

Canada.   At the end of fiscal 2006, we were operating 155 The Home Depot stores in ten Canadian provinces. Of these stores, 20 were opened during fiscal 2006, including two relocations.

Mexico.   At the end of fiscal 2006, we were operating 61 The Home Depot stores in Mexico. Of these stores, seven were opened during fiscal 2006.

China.   In fiscal 2006, we acquired The Home Way, a Chinese home improvement retailer, including 12 stores in six cities.

Credit Services.   We offer credit purchase programs through third-party credit providers to professional, D-I-Y and D-I-F-M customers. In fiscal 2006, approximately 4.5 million new The Home Depot credit accounts were opened, bringing the total number of The Home Depot account holders to approximately 17 million. Proprietary credit card sales accounted for approximately 28% of store sales in fiscal 2006. We also offer an unsecured Home Improvement Loan program through third-party credit providers that gives our customers the opportunity to finance the purchase of products and services in our stores. We believe this loan program not only supports large sales, such as kitchen and bath remodels, but also generates incremental sales from our customers.

Logistics.   Our logistics programs are designed to ensure excellent product availability for customers, effective use of our investment in inventory and low total supply chain costs. At the end of fiscal 2006, we operated 18 import distribution centers located in the U.S. and Canada. At the end of fiscal 2006, we also operated 30 lumber distribution centers in the U.S. and Canada to support the lumber demands of our stores and 10 transit facilities to receive merchandise from manufacturers for immediate delivery to our stores. At the end of fiscal 2006, approximately 40% of the merchandise shipped to our stores flowed through our network of distribution centers and transit facilities. As our networks evolve, we expect to increase our flow-through. The remaining merchandise will be shipped directly from our suppliers to our stores. In addition to replenishing merchandise supplies at our stores, we also provide delivery services directly to our customers.

Seasonality.   Our business is seasonal to a certain extent. Generally, our highest volume of sales occurs in our second fiscal quarter and the lowest volume occurs during our fourth fiscal quarter.

Competition.   Our business is highly competitive, based in part on price, store location, customer service and depth of merchandise. In each of the markets we serve, there are a number of other home improvement stores, electrical, plumbing and building materials supply houses and lumber yards. With respect to some products, we also compete with discount stores, local, regional and national hardware stores, mail order firms, warehouse clubs, independent building supply stores and, to a lesser extent, other retailers. In addition to these entities, our EXPO Design Center stores compete with specialty design stores or showrooms, some of which are only open to interior design professionals. Due to the variety of competition we face, we are unable to precisely measure the impact on our sales by our competitors.

HD Supply Segment

Operating Strategy.   Our operating strategy is to provide a total solution for every phase of a building project, from infrastructure to construction to lifetime maintenance and repair and remodel. We believe that our broad product and service offering, our highly knowledgeable sales force and our reputation for superior customer service enable us to be a single-source supplier to our customers for the entire project lifecycle.

Customers. We distribute products and offer services primarily to builders, contractors, government entities, industrial businesses and maintenance professionals. Our customers typically select their vendors primarily on the basis of product availability, relationships with and expertise of sales personnel, price and the quality and scope of services offered. Additionally, professional customers generally purchase large volumes, are repeat buyers because of their involvement in longer-term projects and require specialized services. We complement our product offering with customer-driven, value-added services, such as integrated supply, design assistance, kitting, assembly and fabrication services.

Products and Services. Our products and services are focused around the following four major categories that are related to different phases of a building project:

- Infrastructure: This category covers the products and services to construct and support the public works systems for residential and commercial projects.

- Construction: This category covers the interior and exterior structural building components for residential and commercial projects.

- Maintenance: This category covers products and services for the routine maintenance, repair and operations needs of multifamily housing, hospitality, healthcare, government and industrial facilities.

- Repair and Remodel: This category covers home improvement products and building materials, serving the consumer, professional handyman and light remodeler markets.

Inventories. We maintain extensive inventories to meet the rapid delivery requirements of our customers. Our inventories are based on the needs, delivery schedules and lead times of our customers. We focus on distributing products that leverage our strengths in inventory management, purchasing, specialized sales force, distribution and logistics, credit management and information technology.

Credit Services. Over 90% of our sales volume is facilitated through the extension of credit to our customers. Our businesses offer credit to customers, either through unsecured credit that is based solely upon the creditworthiness of the customer, or secured credit for materials sold for a specific job where the security lies in lien rights associated with the material going into the job. The type of credit offered depends both on the financial strength of the customer and the nature of the business in which the customer is involved. End users, resellers and other non-contractor customers generally purchase more on unsecured credit than secured credit. These lines of credit are granted only after a sufficient review of the creditworthiness of the customer. In addition, on a regular basis, large unsecured credit lines are reviewed to ensure they are still financially sound.

Logistics. Our distribution network consists of over 1,000 combined branches and central distribution centers in the United States. The efficient operation of our distribution network is critical in providing quality service to our customer base. Our central distribution centers and branches use warehouse management technology to optimize receiving, inventory control and picking, packing and shipping functions. In addition, we leverage several of our larger branches as distribution points for certain product lines.

The majority of customer orders are shipped from inventory at our branches. In order to maintain complete control of the delivery process, we use over 4,000 vehicles from our total vehicle fleet to deliver products to our customers. We also accommodate special orders from our customers and facilitate the shipment of certain large volume orders directly from the manufacturer to the customer. Orders for larger construction projects normally require long-term delivery schedules throughout the period of construction, which in some cases may continue for several years.

Seasonality.   Our business is seasonal to a certain extent. Generally, our highest volume of sales occurs in our second fiscal quarter and the lowest volume occurs during our fourth fiscal quarter.

Competition.   We are one of the largest wholesale distributors of our range of products in the United States, and we believe that no other company competes against us across all of our product lines. However, there is significant competition in each of our individual product lines. Our competition includes other wholesalers, manufacturers that sell products directly to their respective customer base and some of our customers that resell our products. To a limited extent, retailers of plumbing, electrical fixtures and supplies, building materials, maintenance repair and operations supplies and contractors' tools also compete with us. Competition varies depending on product line, customer classification and geographic area. The principal competitive factors in our business include, but are not limited to, availability of materials and supplies; technical product knowledge and expertise as to application and usage; advisory or other service capabilities; ability to build and maintain customer relationships; same-day delivery capabilities in certain product lines; pricing of products and provision of credit.

Support Services

Information Technologies.   During fiscal 2006, we continued to make significant information technology investments to support better customer service and provide an improved shopping environment in our stores. We completed the deployment of self-checkout registers to all our U.S. stores and the majority of our stores in Canada and enhanced our coupon processing at all check-outs. We also began implementing in-store call boxes and installed voice over internet phone systems in order to provide customers faster assistance from our associates. To support the continued growth of our appliance business, we upgraded our proprietary Depot Direct appliance fulfillment system.

In addition to significant investments in store technology, we upgraded our order management system, which improves the speed and accuracy of online order processing and provides customers the ability to check special order status on the internet. We also defined a set of common enterprise system platforms for our HD Supply wholesale businesses and began migrating the HD Supply businesses to these platforms, beginning with the payroll and financial functions.

We also began work on the strategic effort to implement a new Retail Systems platform to further improve the performance of our merchandising functions and store operations. We also commenced the effort to add new automation into our supply chain functions focusing on new systems for warehouse distribution, transportation management and enhancements to support greater order penetration through our centralized replenishment systems.

Associates.   At the end of fiscal 2006, we employed approximately 364,000 associates, of whom approximately 26,000 were salaried, with the remainder compensated on an hourly or temporary basis. Approximately 68% of our associates are employed on a full-time basis. We believe that our employee relations are very good. To attract and retain qualified personnel, we seek to maintain competitive salary and wage levels in each market we serve.

Intellectual Property.   Through our wholly-owned subsidiary, Homer TLC, Inc., we have registered or applied for registration, in a number of countries, for a variety of internet domain names, service marks and trademarks for use in our businesses, including The Home Depot®; HD Supply; Hampton Bay® fans, lighting and accessories; Glacier Bay® toilets, sinks and faucets; Pegasus® faucets and bath accessories; Commercial Electric® lighting fixtures; Workforce® tools, tool boxes and shelving; www.hdsupply.com and www.doitherself.com. Furthermore, we have also obtained and now maintain patent portfolios relating to certain products and services provided by The Home Depot, and continually seek to patent or otherwise protect selected innovations we incorporate into our products and business operations. We regard our intellectual property as having significant value to each business segment and as being an important factor in the marketing of our brand, e-commerce, stores and new areas of business. We are not aware of any facts that could be expected to have a material adverse affect on our intellectual property.

Quality Assurance Program. We have a quality assurance program for our directly imported globally-sourced products. Through this program, we have established criteria for supplier and product performance, which measures factors such as product quality and timeliness of shipments. The performance record is made available to the factories to allow them to strive for improvement. The program addresses quality assurance at the factory, product and packaging levels.

Environmental, Health & Safety ("EH&S"). We are committed to maintaining a safe environment for our customers and associates, and protecting the environment of the communities in which we do business. Our EH&S function in the field is directed by trained associates focused primarily on execution of the EH&S programs. Additionally, we have an Atlanta-based team of dedicated EH&S professionals who evaluate, develop, implement and enforce policies, processes and programs on a Company-wide basis.

Item 1A. Risk Factors.

The risks and uncertainties described below could materially and adversely affect our business, financial condition and results of operations and could cause actual results to differ materially from our expectations and projections. While we believe that our assumptions, expectations and projections are reasonable in view of the currently available information, you are cautioned not to place undue reliance on our forward-looking statements. These statements are not guarantees of future performance. They are subject to future events, risks and uncertainties – many of which are beyond our control – as well as potentially inaccurate assumptions that could cause actual results to differ materially from our expectations and projections. Forward-looking statements may relate to such matters as Net Sales growth, comparable store sales, impact of cannibalization, state of the residential construction and housing markets, commodity price inflation and deflation, implementation of store initiatives, protection of intellectual property rights, Net Earnings performance, including Depreciation and Amortization expense, earnings per share, stock-based compensation expense, store openings and closures, capital allocation and expenditures, the effect of adopting certain accounting standards, return on invested capital, management of our purchasing or customer credit policies, strategic direction, including whether or not a sale or initial public offering of HD Supply will occur or, if a transaction is undertaken, its terms or timing, and the demand for our products and services. You should read these Risk Factors in conjunction with "Management's Discussion and Analysis of Financial Condition and Results of Operations" in Item 7 of this report and our Consolidated Financial Statements and related notes in Item 8 of this report. There also may be other factors that we cannot anticipate or that are not described in this report, generally because we do not perceive them to be material, that could cause results to differ materially from our expectations. Forward-looking statements speak only as of the date they are made, and we do not undertake to update these forward-looking statements. You are advised, however, to review any further disclosures we make on related subjects in our periodic filings with the SEC.

Rising costs, a reduction in the availability of financing, weather and other conditions in North America could adversely affect our costs of doing business, demand for our products and services and our average ticket price.

Interest rates, fuel and other energy costs, labor and healthcare costs, availability of financing, employment, state of the residential construction and housing markets, consumer confidence and general economic outlook, weather, natural disasters, terrorism and other conditions that adversely affect consumer demand for our products and services could adversely affect our financial performance. These and other similar factors could:

- increase our costs,
- cause our customers to delay undertaking or determine not to undertake new home improvement projects,
- cause our customers to delay purchasing or determine not to purchase home improvement products and services,
- cause our customers to delay or determine not to undertake new spending in the commercial, residential, industrial and public infrastructure markets, and
- lead to a decline in customer transactions and in average ticket price.

We rely on third party suppliers, and if we fail to identify and develop relationships with a sufficient number of qualified suppliers, our ability to timely and efficiently access products that meet our high standards for quality could be adversely affected.

We buy our products and supplies from suppliers located throughout the world. Our ability to continue to identify and develop relationships with qualified suppliers who can satisfy our high standards for quality and our need to access products and supplies in a timely and efficient manner is a significant challenge. Our ability to access products and supplies also can be adversely affected by political instability, the financial instability of suppliers, suppliers' noncompliance with applicable laws, trade restrictions, tariffs, currency exchange rates, transport capacity and cost and other factors beyond our control.

If we are unable to effectively manage and expand our alliances and relationships with selected suppliers of brand name products, we may be unable to effectively execute our strategy to differentiate us from our competitors.

As part of our strategy of differentiation, we have formed strategic alliances and exclusive relationships with selected suppliers to market products under a variety of well-recognized brand names. If we are unable to manage and expand these alliances and relationships or identify alternative sources for comparable products, we may not be able to effectively execute our strategy of differentiation.

Any inability to open new stores on schedule will delay the contribution of these new stores to our financial performance.

We expect to increase our presence in existing markets and enter new markets. Our ability to open new stores will depend primarily on our ability to:

- identify attractive locations,
- negotiate leases or real estate purchase agreements on acceptable terms,
- attract and train qualified employees, and
- manage pre-opening expenses, including construction costs.

Our ability to open new stores also will be affected by environmental regulations, local zoning issues and other laws related to land use. Failure to effectively manage these and other similar factors will affect our ability to open stores on schedule, which will delay the impact of these new stores on our financial performance.

The implementation of our technology initiatives could disrupt our operations in the near term, and our technology initiatives might not provide the anticipated benefits or might fail.

We have made, and will continue to make, significant technology investments both in our stores and branches and in our administrative functions. Our technology initiatives are designed to streamline our operations to allow our associates to continue to provide high quality service to our customers and to provide our customers a better experience. The cost and potential problems and interruptions associated with the implementation of our technology initiatives could disrupt or reduce the efficiency of our operations in the near term. In addition, our new or upgraded technology might not provide the anticipated benefits, it might take longer than expected to realize the anticipated benefits or the technology might fail altogether.

We may not timely identify or effectively respond to consumer trends, which could adversely affect our relationship with our customers, the demand for our products and services and our market share.

It is difficult to successfully predict the products and services our customers will demand. The success of our business depends in part on our ability to identify and respond to evolving trends in demographics and consumer preferences. Failure to design attractive stores and to timely identify or effectively respond to changing consumer tastes, preferences, spending patterns and home improvement needs could adversely affect our relationship with our customers, the demand for our products and services and our market share.

The inflation or deflation of commodity prices could affect our prices, demand for our products, sales and profit margins.

Prices of certain commodity products, including lumber and other raw materials, are historically volatile and are subject to fluctuations arising from changes in domestic and international supply and demand, labor costs, competition, market speculation, government regulations and periodic delays in delivery. Rapid and significant changes in commodity prices may affect our sales and profit margins.

If we cannot successfully manage the unique challenges presented by international markets, we may not be successful in expanding our international operations.

Our strategy includes expansion of our operations in existing and new international markets by selective acquisitions, strategic alliances and the opening of new stores and branches. Our ability to successfully execute our strategy in international markets is affected by many of the same operational risks we face in expanding our U.S. operations. In addition, our international expansion may be adversely affected by our ability to identify and gain access to local suppliers as well as by local laws and customs, legal and regulatory constraints, political and economic conditions and currency regulations of the countries or regions in which we currently operate or intend to operate in the future. Risks inherent in our international operations also include, among others, the costs and difficulties of managing international operations, adverse tax consequences and greater difficulty in enforcing intellectual property rights. Additionally, foreign currency exchange rates and fluctuations may have an impact on our future costs or on future cash flows from our international operations.

Our success depends upon our ability to attract, train and retain highly qualified associates.

To be successful, we must attract, train and retain a large and growing number of highly qualified associates while controlling related labor costs. Our ability to control labor costs is subject to numerous external factors, including prevailing wage rates and health and other insurance costs. In addition, many of our associates are in hourly positions with historically high turnover rates. We compete with other retail and non-retail businesses for these associates and invest significant resources in training and motivating them. We also depend on our executives and other key associates for our success. There is no assurance that we will be able to attract or retain highly qualified associates in the future.

Changes in accounting standards and subjective assumptions, estimates and judgments by management related to complex accounting matters could significantly affect our financial results.

Generally accepted accounting principles and related accounting pronouncements, implementation guidelines and interpretations with regard to a wide range of matters that are relevant to our business, such as revenue recognition, asset impairment, inventories, self-insurance, tax matters and litigation, are highly complex and involve many subjective assumptions, estimates and judgments by our management. Changes in these rules or their interpretation or changes in underlying assumptions, estimates or judgments by our management could significantly change our reported or expected financial performance.

Increased competition could adversely affect prices and demand for our products and services and could decrease our market share.

We operate in markets in industries that are highly competitive. Our retail business competes principally based on price, store location, customer service and depth of merchandise. Our HD Supply business competes principally based on ability to provide and deliver supplies, product knowledge and expertise, advisory services and availability of credit. In each market we serve, there are a number of other home improvement stores, electrical, plumbing and building materials supply houses and lumber yards. With respect to some products, we also compete with discount stores, local, regional and national hardware stores, mail order firms, warehouse clubs, independent building supply stores and other retailers. In addition, we compete with specialty design stores or showrooms, some of which are only open to interior design professionals, local and regional distributors, and wholesalers and manufacturers that sell products directly to their customer bases. Intense competitive pressures from one or more of our competitors could affect prices or demand for our products and services. If we are unable to timely and appropriately respond to these pressures, our financial performance and our market share could be adversely affected.

We are involved in a number of legal proceedings, and while we cannot predict the outcomes of such proceedings and other contingencies with certainty, some of these outcomes may adversely affect our operations or increase our costs.

We are involved in a number of legal proceedings, including government inquiries and investigations, and consumer, employment, tort and other litigation. We cannot predict the outcomes of these legal proceedings and other contingencies, including environmental remediation and other proceedings commenced by government authorities, with certainty. The outcome of some of these legal proceedings and other contingencies could require us to take or refrain from taking actions which could adversely affect our operations or could require us to pay substantial amounts of money. Additionally, defending against these lawsuits and proceedings may involve significant expense and diversion of management's attention and resources from other matters.

Our costs of doing business could increase as a result of changes in federal, state or local regulations.

Changes in the federal, state or local minimum wage or living wage requirements or changes in other wage or workplace regulations could increase our costs of doing business. Changes in federal, state or local regulations governing the sale of some of our products could increase our costs of doing business. In addition, changes to federal, state and local tax regulations could increase our costs of doing business.

Item 1B. Unresolved Staff Comments.

Not applicable.

Item 2. Properties.

The following tables show locations of the 1,872 The Home Depot stores and the 830 HD Supply locations in the U.S. and its territories and the 228 The Home Depot stores and the 63 HD Supply locations outside of the U.S. at the end of fiscal 2006:

U.S. Locations	Number of Locations		U.S. Locations	Number of Locations	
	Retail	HD Supply		Retail	HD Supply
Alabama	26	8	Nebraska	8	4
Alaska	6	1	Nevada	17	12
Arizona	52	51	New Hampshire	19	—
Arkansas	14	8	New Jersey	64	7
California	214	99	New Mexico	13	8
Colorado	44	23	New York	97	1
Connecticut	26	—	North Carolina	41	46
Delaware	7	6	North Dakota	2	—
District of Columbia	1	—	Ohio	70	31
Florida	140	123	Oklahoma	16	2
Georgia	81	81	Oregon	22	8
Hawaii	7	3	Pennsylvania	66	7
Idaho	11	3	Puerto Rico	8	—
Illinois	70	15	Rhode Island	8	1
Indiana	26	13	South Carolina	25	30
Iowa	9	5	South Dakota	1	—
Kansas	16	4	Tennessee	34	24
Kentucky	15	7	Texas	172	71
Louisiana	25	11	Utah	19	8
Maine	11	—	Vermont	4	—
Maryland	40	19	Virgin Islands	1	—
Massachusetts	42	2	Virginia	45	20
Michigan	70	6	Washington	42	20
Minnesota	31	3	West Virginia	6	4
Mississippi	14	12	Wisconsin	30	3
Missouri	33	11	Wyoming	5	4
Montana	6	5	Total U.S.	1,872	830

International Locations	Number of Locations	
	Retail	HD Supply
Canada:		
Alberta	21	3
British Columbia	22	5
Manitoba	6	2
New Brunswick	3	1
Newfoundland	1	—
Nova Scotia	3	2
Ontario	75	46
Prince Edward Island	1	1
Quebec	20	2
Saskatchewan	3	1
Total Canada	155	63
China:		
Beijing	2	
Henan	1	
Liaoning	1	
Shaanxi	2	
Shandong	1	
Tianjin	5	
Total China	12	

International Locations	Number of Locations
	Retail
Mexico:	
Aguascalientes	1
Baja California	3
Baja California Sur	1
Chihuahua	5
Coahuila	2
Distrito Federal	7
Durango	1
Guanajuato	4
Guerrero	1
Hidalgo	1
Jalisco	3
Michoacán	1
Morelos	1
Nuevo León	6
Puebla	2
Queretaro	1
Quintana Roo	1
San Luis Potosi	1
Sinaloa	3
Sonora	2
State of Mexico	8
Tabasco	1
Tamaulipas	2
Veracruz	2
Yucatan	1
Total Mexico	61

Additionally, at the end of fiscal 2006, we had 47 other retail store locations, which included 34 EXPO Design Center stores located in Arizona, California, Florida, Georgia, Illinois, Maryland, Massachusetts, Missouri, New Jersey, New York, Tennessee, Texas and Virginia; 11 The Home Depot Landscape Supply stores located in Georgia and Texas; and two The Home Depot Floor Stores located in Florida and Texas. We also operated seven Home Decorators Collection locations in Illinois, Kansas, Missouri and Oklahoma.

Of our 2,147 retail stores at the end of fiscal 2006, approximately 87% were owned (including those owned subject to a ground lease) consisting of approximately 196.0 million square feet, and approximately 13% of such stores were leased consisting of approximately 29.3 million square feet. In recent years, we have increased the relative percentage of new stores that are owned. We generally prefer to own retail stores because of greater operating control and flexibility, generally lower occupancy costs and certain other economic advantages.

At the end of fiscal 2006, our Retail segment utilized 195 warehouses and distribution centers located in 42 states, consisting of approximately 28.2 million square feet, of which approximately 2.0 million is owned and approximately 26.2 million is leased.

HD Supply consists of four major platforms: infrastructure, construction, maintenance and repair and remodel. The infrastructure platform consists of 325 U.S. branches in 41 states and four branches in Canada. The construction platform consists of 527 U.S. branches in 35 states and 56 branches in Canada. The maintenance platform consists of 90 U.S. branches in 25 states and five branches in Canada. Finally, the repair and remodel platform consists of 13 U.S. branches in two states. One or more platforms may operate multiple branches at one HD Supply location.

Of our 893 HD Supply locations at the end of fiscal 2006, approximately 13% were owned (including those owned subject to a ground lease) and approximately 87% of such stores were leased. We generally prefer to lease HD Supply locations as it provides flexibility to relocate or expand with our HD Supply customer base. Additionally, HD Supply had 66 U.S. warehouses and distribution centers located in 19 states and two in Canada to support other HD Supply locations. The HD Supply locations, warehouses and distribution centers utilized approximately 23.7 million square feet, of which approximately 2.8 million is owned and approximately 20.9 million is leased at the end of fiscal 2006.

Our executive, corporate staff, divisional staff and financial offices occupy approximately 2.0 million square feet of leased and owned space in Atlanta, Georgia. At the end of fiscal 2006, we occupied an aggregate of approximately 4.4 million square feet, of which approximately 2.5 million square feet is owned and approximately 1.9 million square feet is leased, for store support centers and customer support centers.

We believe that at the end of existing lease terms, our current leased space can be either relet or replaced by alternate space for lease or purchase that is readily available.

Item 3. Legal Proceedings.

In August 2005, the Company received an informal request from the staff of the SEC for information related to the Company's return-to-vendor policies and procedures. The Company has responded to this and subsequent requests and continues to fully cooperate with the SEC staff. The SEC has informed the Company that the informal inquiry is not an indication that any violations of law have occurred. Although the Company cannot predict the outcome of this matter, it does not expect that this informal inquiry will have a material adverse effect on its consolidated financial condition or results of operations.

In June 2006, the SEC commenced an informal inquiry into the Company's stock option granting practices, and the Office of the U.S. Attorney for the Southern District of New York has also requested information on this subject. In addition, a subcommittee of the Audit Committee reviewed the Company's historical stock option practices and engaged independent outside counsel to assist in this matter. On December 6, 2006, the Company announced the results of this investigation. The Company determined that the unrecorded expense from 1981 through the present is approximately $227 million in the aggregate, including related tax items. In accordance with the provisions of Staff Accounting Bulletin No. 108, "Considering the Effects of Prior Year Misstatements when Quantifying Misstatements in Current Year Financial Statements," the Company corrected these errors by decreasing beginning Retained Earnings for fiscal 2006 by $227 million, with offsetting entries to Paid-In Capital, Other Accrued Expenses and Deferred Income Taxes, within its Consolidated Financial Statements. The Company and the subcommittee are continuing to cooperate with the SEC and the Office of U.S. Attorney. Although the Company cannot predict the outcome of these matters, it does not believe they will have a material adverse effect on its consolidated financial condition or results of operations.

The following actions have been filed against the Company and, in some cases, against certain of its current and former officers and directors as described below. Although the Company cannot predict their outcome, it does not expect these actions, individually or together, will have a material adverse effect on its consolidated financial condition or results of operations.

In the second quarter of fiscal 2006, six purported, but as yet uncertified, class actions were filed against the Company and certain of its current and former officers and directors in the U.S. District Court for the Northern District of Georgia in Atlanta, alleging certain misrepresentations in violation of Sections 10(b) and 20(a) of the Securities Exchange Act of 1934 and Rule 10b-5 thereunder in connection with the Company's return-to-vendor practices. These actions were filed by certain current and former shareholders of the Company. In the third quarter of fiscal 2006, one of the shareholders dismissed his complaint. The Court has preliminarily appointed a lead plaintiff, and the lead plaintiff has filed an amended complaint in each of the remaining five actions. Relief sought in the amended complaint includes unspecified damages and costs and attorney's fees. The defendants have filed a motion to dismiss the amended complaint. The Company believes these actions are without merit and intends to defend them vigorously.

In the second and third quarters of fiscal 2006, three purported, but as yet uncertified, class actions were filed against the Company, The Home Depot FutureBuilder Administrative Committee and certain of the Company's current and former directors and employees in federal court in Brooklyn, New York alleging breach of fiduciary duty in violation of the Employee Retirement Income Security Act of 1974 in connection with the Company's return-to-vendor and stock option practices. These actions were transferred to the U.S. District Court for the Northern District of Georgia in Atlanta. These actions were brought by certain former employees of the Company and seek unspecified damages, costs, attorneys' fees and equitable and injunctive relief. The Company believes these actions are without merit and intends to defend them vigorously.

In the second and third quarters of fiscal 2006, six shareholder derivative actions were filed nominally on behalf of the Company against certain current and former officers and directors in the Superior Court of Fulton County, Georgia, alleging breach of fiduciary duty, abuse of control, gross mismanagement, waste of corporate assets, and unjust enrichment in connection with the Company's return-to-vendor, stock option, and compensation practices. Such actions were filed by alleged shareholders of the Company. Relief sought in each action includes unspecified damages, injunctive relief, disgorgement of profits, benefits and compensation obtained by the defendants, costs, and attorney's fees. Subsequently, one joint amended complaint was filed on behalf of all plaintiffs encompassing all the various claims and seeking the same relief. The defendants have moved to dismiss or alternatively stay the litigation.

In the first quarter of fiscal 2007, one additional shareholder derivative action was filed nominally on behalf of the Company against certain of the Company's current directors and its former chief executive officer in the U.S. District Court for the Northern District of Georgia in Atlanta, alleging breach of fiduciary duty, abuse of control, gross mismanagement, waste of corporate assets and unjust enrichment in connection with the Company's stock option and compensation practices. The action was filed by alleged shareholders of the Company. Relief sought in the action includes unspecified damages, injunctive relief, punitive damages, and costs and attorneys' fees.

In compliance with SEC disclosure requirements, the environmental proceedings set forth below involve potential monetary sanctions of $100,000 or more. Although the Company cannot predict the outcome of these proceedings, it does not expect any such outcome to have a material adverse effect on its consolidated financial condition or results of operations.

In January 2003, Home Depot U.S.A., Inc., a wholly-owned subsidiary of the Company, received a request for information from the U.S. Environmental Protection Agency ("EPA") regarding alleged pollutant discharges during construction activities at certain The Home Depot stores. The EPA subsequently referred this matter to the U.S. Department of Justice ("DOJ"). The DOJ and the Company are currently discussing the potential settlement of this matter.

In April 2005, the Company received subpoenas from the State of New York's Office of Attorney General seeking documents and testimony related to the sale and handling of pesticides. The Company is cooperating fully with the Office of Attorney General and believes it is indemnified if monetary sanctions are imposed.

In July 2005, the Company received a grand jury subpoena from the United States Attorney's Office in Los Angeles, California, seeking documents and information relating to the Company's handling, storage and disposal of hazardous waste. California state and local government authorities are also

14

investigating this matter. In January 2006, the Company received an administrative subpoena from the District Attorney of Riverside County, California seeking records and documents in connection with such investigation. The Company is cooperating fully with the respective authorities. The California state and local authorities and the Company are currently discussing the potential settlement of this matter.

Item 4. Submission of Matters to a Vote of Security Holders.

Not applicable.

Item 4A. Executive Officers of the Company.

Executive officers of the Company are appointed by, and serve at the pleasure of, the Board of Directors. The current executive officers of the Company are as follows:

ROGER W. ADAMS, age 50, has been Senior Vice President and Chief Marketing Officer since October 2006. From February 2005 through October 2006, he served as the Company's Senior Vice President – Marketing. Mr. Adams previously served as Executive Director of Corporate Advertising, Marketing and CRM of General Motors Corporation from June 2004 to January 2005. From March 1996 to June 2004, he served as general manager of General Motor's Buick, Pontiac and GMC Division.

FRANCIS S. BLAKE, age 57, has been Chairman and Chief Executive Officer since January 2007. From March 2002 through January 2007, he served as the Company's Executive Vice President – Business Development and Corporate Operations. He was formerly the Deputy Secretary of Energy from June 2001 until March 2002. From June 2000 until May 2001, he was a Senior Vice President at General Electric Company and was Vice President of GE Power Systems from February 1996 until July 2000. Mr. Blake serves as a director of The Southern Company.

TIMOTHY M. CROW, age 51, has been Executive Vice President – Human Resources since February 2007. From May 2002 to February 2007, he served as Senior Vice President, Organization, Talent and Performance Systems. Mr. Crow previously served as Senior Vice President – Human Resources of K-Mart Corporation, a mass merchandising company, from 1999 through May 2002.

JOSEPH J. DeANGELO, age 45, has been Executive Vice President and Chief Operating Officer since January 2007. From August 2005 through December 2006, he served as the Company's Executive Vice President – Home Depot Supply. From January 2005 through August 2005, he served as Senior Vice President – Home Depot Supply, Pro Business and Tool Rental, and from April 2004 through January 2005, he served as Senior Vice President – Pro Business and Tool Rental. Mr. DeAngelo previously served as Executive Vice President of The Stanley Works, a tool manufacturing company, from April 2003 through April 2004. From 1986 until April 2003, Mr. DeAngelo held various positions with General Electric Company. His final position with GE was as President and Chief Executive Officer of GE TIP/Modular Space, a division of GE Capital.

ROBERT P. DeRODES, age 56, has been Executive Vice President – Chief Information Officer since February 2002. He previously served as President and Chief Executive Officer of Delta Technology, Inc. and Chief Information Officer for Delta Air Lines, Inc. from September 1999 until February 2002. From February 1995 to September 1999, he served as Senior Technology Officer at Citibank for the Card Products Group. From February 1993 to February 1995, he was President of Sabre Development Services for the Sabre Group Holdings, Inc., a subsidiary of American Airlines, Inc.

MARVIN R. ELLISON, age 42, has been President – Northern Division since January 2006. From August 2005 through January 2006, he served as Senior Vice President – Logistics and from October 2004 through August 2005 he served as Vice President – Logistics. From June 2002 through October 2004, he served as Vice President – Loss Prevention. From 1987 until June 2002, Mr. Ellison held various management and executive level positions with Target Corporation, a general merchandise retailer. His final position with Target was Director, Assets Protection.

CRAIG A. MENEAR, age 49, has been Senior Vice President – Merchandising since October 2006. From August 2003 through October 2006, he has served as Senior Vice President – Merchandising, Hardlines. From 1997 through August 2003, Mr. Menear served in various management and vice president level positions in the Company's Merchandising department, including Merchandising Vice President of Hardware, Merchandising Vice President of the Southwest Division, and Divisional Merchandise Manager of the Southwest Division.

BRUCE A. MERINO, age 53, has been President – Western Division since May 2000 and President, EXPO Design Center since October 2005. From October 1996 through May 2000, he served as Merchandising Vice President.

PAUL RAINES, age 42, has been President – Southern Division since February 2005. Prior thereto he served as Regional Vice President – Florida from April 2003 through January 2005. From January 2002 through April 2003, Mr. Raines served as Vice President – Store Operations, and from January 2000 through January 2002, Mr. Raines served as Director of Labor Management.

RICARDO SALVIDAR, age 54, has been President – Mexico since 2001. From 1980 to 2001, Mr. Salvidar held various management and executive level positions with Grupo Alfa, a Mexican conglomerate. His final position with Grupo Alfa was President and Chief Executive Officer of Total Home.

JAMES C. SNYDER, JR., age 43, has been Vice President – Secretary and Acting General Counsel since February 2007. From March 2006 to February 2007, Mr. Snyder served as Vice President – Legal, Risk Management. From March 2004 to March 2006 Mr. Snyder served as Vice President – Legal. Prior thereto Mr. Snyder served as Director, Legal from November 2002 to March 2004. Mr. Snyder joined the Company in March 2001 as Corporate Counsel.

CAROL B. TOMÉ, age 50, has been Chief Financial Officer since May 2001 and Executive Vice President – Corporate Services since January 2007. Prior thereto Ms. Tomé served as Senior Vice President – Finance and Accounting/Treasurer from February 2000 through May 2001 and as Vice President and Treasurer from 1995 through February 2000. From 1992 until 1995, when she joined the Company, Ms. Tomé was Vice President and Treasurer of Riverwood International Corporation, a provider of paperboard packaging. Ms. Tomé serves as a director of United Parcel Service, Inc.

ANNETTE M. VERSCHUREN, age 50, has been President, The Home Depot Canada since March 1996 and President, The Home Depot Asia since September 2006. From February 2003 through October 2005, she also served as President, EXPO Design Center.

PART II

Item 5. Market for Registrant's Common Equity, Related Stockholder Matters and Issuer Purchases of Equity Securities.

Since April 19, 1984, our common stock has been listed on the New York Stock Exchange, trading under the symbol "HD." The Company paid its first cash dividend on June 22, 1987, and has paid cash dividends during each subsequent quarter. Future dividend payments will depend on the Company's earnings, capital requirements, financial condition and other factors considered relevant by the Board of Directors.

The table below sets forth the high and low sales prices of our common stock on the New York Stock Exchange and the quarterly cash dividends declared per share of common stock during the periods indicated.

	Price Range		Cash Dividends Declared
	High	Low	
Fiscal Year 2006			
First Quarter Ended April 30, 2006	$43.95	$38.50	$0.150
Second Quarter Ended July 30, 2006	$41.61	$32.85	$0.150
Third Quarter Ended October 29, 2006	$38.24	$33.07	$0.225
Fourth Quarter Ended January 28, 2007	$41.84	$35.77	$0.225
Fiscal Year 2005			
First Quarter Ended May 1, 2005	$42.99	$34.56	$0.100
Second Quarter Ended July 31, 2005	$43.98	$35.54	$0.100
Third Quarter Ended October 30, 2005	$43.39	$37.14	$0.100
Fourth Quarter Ended January 29, 2006	$43.27	$39.65	$0.150

As of March 26, 2007, there were approximately 180,000 shareholders of record and approximately 1,700,000 additional shareholders holding stock under nominee security position listings.

Stock Performance Graph

This graph depicts the Company's cumulative total shareholder returns relative to the performance of the Standard & Poor's 500 Composite Stock Index and the Standard & Poor's Retail Composite Index for the five-year period commencing February 4, 2002, the first trading day of Fiscal 2002, and ending on January 26, 2007, the last trading day of Fiscal 2006. The graph assumes $100 invested at the closing price of the Company's common stock on the New York Stock Exchange and each index on February 1, 2002 and assumes that all dividends were reinvested on the date paid. The points on the graph represent fiscal year-end amounts based on the last trading day in each fiscal year.

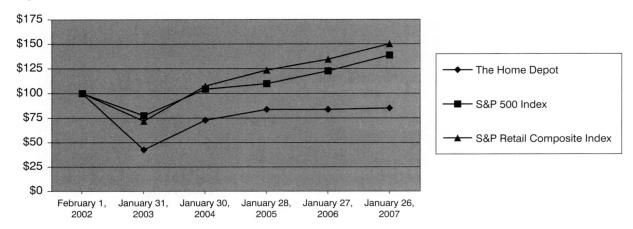

	Fiscal 2001	Fiscal 2002	Fiscal 2003	Fiscal 2004	Fiscal 2005	Fiscal 2006
The Home Depot	$100.00	$42.57	$ 72.88	$ 83.75	$ 83.72	$ 85.12
S&P 500 Index	$100.00	$77.53	$104.34	$109.90	$122.67	$138.49
S&P Retail Composite Index	$100.00	$71.95	$107.54	$123.56	$134.39	$150.06

Issuer Purchases of Equity Securities

Since fiscal 2002, the Company has repurchased shares of its common stock having a value of approximately $16.4 billion. The number and average price of shares purchased in each fiscal month of the fourth quarter of fiscal 2006 are set forth in the table below:

Period	Total Number of Shares Purchased[1]	Average Price Paid per Share	Total Number of Shares Purchased as Part of Publicly Announced Program[2]	Approximate Dollar Value of Shares that May Yet Be Purchased Under the Program
Oct. 30, 2006 – Nov. 26, 2006	3,331,219	$36.93	3,294,598	$4,116,600,751
Nov. 27, 2006 – Dec. 24, 2006	75,065,717	$39.97	75,056,293	$1,116,575,324
Dec. 25, 2006 – Jan. 28, 2007	295,277	$40.39	—	$1,116,575,324

(1) These amounts include repurchases pursuant to the Company's 1997 and 2005 Omnibus Stock Incentive Plans (the "Plans"). Under the Plans, participants may exercise stock options by surrendering shares of common stock that the participants already own as payment of the exercise price. Participants in the Plans may also surrender shares as payment of applicable tax withholding on the vesting of restricted stock and deferred share awards. Shares so surrendered by participants in the Plans are repurchased pursuant to the terms of the Plans and applicable award agreement and not pursuant to publicly announced share repurchase programs. For the quarter ended January 28, 2007, the following shares of The Home Depot common stock were surrendered by participants in the Plans and included in the total number of shares purchased: Oct. 30, 2006 – Nov. 26, 2006 – 36,621 shares at an average price per share of $37.82; Nov. 27, 2006 – Dec. 24, 2006 – 9,424 shares at an average price per share of $39.35; Dec. 25, 2006 – Jan. 28, 2007 – 295,277 shares at an average price per share of $40.39.

(2) The Company's common stock repurchase program was initially announced on July 15, 2002. As of the end of the fourth quarter of fiscal 2006, the Board had approved purchases up to $17.5 billion. The program does not have a prescribed expiration date.

Sales of Unregistered Securities

During the fourth quarter of fiscal 2006, the Company issued 5,805 deferred stock units under The Home Depot, Inc. NonEmployee Directors' Deferred Stock Compensation Plan pursuant to the exemption from registration provided by Section 4(2) of the Securities Act of 1933, as amended. The deferred stock units were credited to the accounts of such nonemployee directors who elected to receive board and committee fees in the form of deferred stock units instead of receiving such fees in cash as payment for board and committee meetings held during the fourth quarter of fiscal 2006. The deferred stock units convert to shares of common stock on a one-for-one basis following a termination of service as described in this plan.

During the fourth quarter of fiscal 2006, the Company credited 884 deferred stock units to participant accounts under The Home Depot FutureBuilder Restoration Plan pursuant to an exemption from the registration requirements of the Securities Act of 1933, as amended, for involuntary, non-contributory plans. The deferred stock units convert to shares of common stock on a one-for-one basis following the termination of services as described in this plan.

Item 6. Selected Financial Data.

The information required by this item is incorporated by reference to pages F-1 and F-2 of this report.

Item 7. Management's Discussion and Analysis of Financial Condition and Results of Operations.

Executive Summary and Selected Consolidated Statements of Earnings Data

For fiscal year ended January 28, 2007 ("fiscal 2006"), we reported Net Earnings of $5.8 billion and Diluted Earnings per Share of $2.79 compared to Net Earnings of $5.8 billion and Diluted Earnings per Share of $2.72 for fiscal year ended January 29, 2006 ("fiscal 2005"). Net Sales increased 11.4% to $90.8 billion for fiscal 2006 from $81.5 billion for fiscal 2005. Our gross profit margin was 32.8% and our operating margin was 10.7% for fiscal 2006.

In the face of a slowdown in the housing market, our retail comparable store sales declined 2.8% in fiscal 2006 driven by a decline in comparable store customer transactions. This was partially offset by an increase in our average ticket of 1.6% in fiscal 2006 to $58.90, including increases in 8 of 10 selling departments.

We grew our numerous installation and home maintenance programs serving our do-it-for-me customers through our stores. Our retail services revenue increased 8.3% to $3.8 billion for fiscal 2006. We experienced sustained growth in categories such as countertops, exterior patios, solar, windows and HVAC.

We continued to introduce innovative and distinctive merchandise that reflects emerging consumer trends, supported by continued investments in store modernization and technology. We invested $3.5 billion in capital expenditures during fiscal 2006 primarily for new store construction, store modernization and technology. We began an accelerated store reinvestment program whereby we increased our investment in existing stores by $350 million more than our plan in the second half of fiscal 2006 to enhance the customer experience. This investment included capital and expense dollars to reset 100 merchandise bays in 540 stores, incorporate a richer staffing model and support our "Orange Juiced" program, a customer service incentive program for our store associates.

We added 125 new stores in fiscal 2006, including 12 stores through our acquisition of The Home Way, a Chinese home improvement retailer, and 10 relocations, bringing our total store count at the end of fiscal 2006 to 2,147. As of the end of fiscal 2006, 228, or approximately 11%, of our stores were located in Canada, Mexico or China compared to 191, or approximately 9%, at the end of fiscal 2005.

We have expanded our business by capturing a growing share of the professional residential, commercial and heavy construction markets through the growth of HD Supply. HD Supply experienced 162% Net Sales growth in fiscal 2006 and accounted for approximately 13% of our total Net Sales in fiscal 2006. We completed 12 acquisitions in fiscal 2006 that were integrated into HD Supply, including Hughes Supply, Inc., a leading distributor of construction and repair products. Organic Net Sales growth for the HD Supply segment was 5.6% in fiscal 2006.

In February 2007, we announced our decision to evaluate strategic alternatives for HD Supply. In order to maximize the value of HD Supply, we would need to further integrate it with our Retail business. We are currently evaluating whether this integration or other strategic alternatives, such as a sale or initial public offering of the business, would create the most shareholder value.

We generated $7.7 billion of cash flow from operations in fiscal 2006. We used this cash flow, along with the net proceeds of additional borrowings of $7.6 billion, to fund $8.1 billion of share repurchases and dividends, $4.3 billion in acquisitions and $3.5 billion in capital expenditures. At the end of fiscal 2006, our long-term debt-to-equity ratio was 47%. Our return on invested capital (computed on beginning long-term debt and equity for the trailing four quarters) was 20.5% at the end of fiscal 2006 compared to 22.4% for fiscal 2005.

We believe the selected sales data, the percentage relationship between Net Sales and major categories in the Consolidated Statements of Earnings and the percentage change in the dollar amounts of each of the items presented as follows is important in evaluating the performance of our business operations.

| | % of Net Sales | | | % Increase (Decrease) In Dollar Amounts | |
| | Fiscal Year[1] | | | | |
	2006	2005	2004	2006 vs. 2005	2005 vs. 2004
NET SALES	**100.0%**	100.0%	100.0%	11.4%	11.5%
Gross Profit	**32.8**	33.5	33.4	9.0	11.8
Operating Expenses:					
Selling, General and Administrative	**20.2**	20.2	20.9	11.3	8.1
Depreciation and Amortization	**1.9**	1.8	1.7	19.7	17.9
Total Operating Expenses	**22.1**	22.0	22.6	12.0	8.8
OPERATING INCOME	**10.7**	11.5	10.8	3.3	18.1
Interest Income (Expense):					
Interest and Investment Income	**—**	0.1	0.1	(56.5)	10.7
Interest Expense	**(0.4)**	(0.2)	(0.1)	174.1	104.3
Interest, net	**(0.4)**	(0.1)	—	350.6	478.6
EARNINGS BEFORE PROVISION FOR INCOME TAXES	**10.3**	11.4	10.8	0.3	17.3
Provision for Income Taxes	**4.0**	4.2	4.0	3.0	18.3
NET EARNINGS	**6.3%**	7.2%	6.8%	(1.3)%	16.7%
SELECTED SALES DATA[2]					
Number of Retail Customer Transactions (millions)	**1,330**	1,330	1,295	0.0%	2.7%
Average Ticket	**$ 58.90**	$ 57.98	$ 54.89	1.6	5.6
Weighted Average Weekly Sales per Operating Store (000s)	**$ 723**	$ 763	$ 766	(5.2)	(0.4)
Weighted Average Sales per Square Foot	**$357.83**	$377.01	$375.26	(5.1)	0.5
Retail Comparable Store Sales (Decrease) Increase (%)[3]	**(2.8)%**	3.1%	5.1%	N/A	N/A

(1) Fiscal years 2006, 2005 and 2004 refer to the fiscal years ended January 28, 2007, January 29, 2006 and January 30, 2005, respectively. Fiscal years 2006, 2005 and 2004 include 52 weeks.

(2) Includes Retail segment only.

(3) Includes Net Sales at locations open greater than 12 months, including relocated and remodeled stores. Retail stores become comparable on the Monday following their 365th day of operation. Retail comparable store sales is intended only as supplemental information and is not a substitute for Net Sales or Net Earnings presented in accordance with generally accepted accounting principles.

Results of Operations

For an understanding of the significant factors that influenced our performance during the past three fiscal years, the following discussion should be read in conjunction with the Consolidated Financial Statements and the Notes to Consolidated Financial Statements presented in this report.

We operate in two reportable business segments: Retail and HD Supply. The Retail segment is principally engaged in the operation of retail stores located in the United States, Canada, Mexico and our recently acquired stores in China. The HD Supply segment distributes products and sells installation services to business-to-business customers, including home builders, professional contractors, municipalities and maintenance professionals. We identify segments based on how management makes operating decisions, assesses performance and allocates resources. The first quarter of fiscal 2006 was the first period in which we began to report our results of operations in two segments. This change was a result of the purchase of Hughes Supply, which significantly increased the size of HD Supply and resulted in changes in our internal reporting and management structure.

The Retail segment includes The Home Depot stores, EXPO Design Center stores ("EXPO") and other retail formats. The Retail segment also includes our retail services business and our catalog and on-line sales businesses.

The HD Supply segment consists of four major platforms: 1) infrastructure, including waterworks and utilities; 2) construction, including construction supply, lumber and building materials, electrical, plumbing/HVAC and interiors; 3) maintenance, including facilities maintenance and industrial PVF; and 4) repair and remodel.

Fiscal 2006 Compared to Fiscal 2005

Net Sales

Total Net Sales for fiscal 2006 increased 11.4%, or $9.3 billion, to $90.8 billion from $81.5 billion for fiscal 2005. Of the $9.3 billion increase, $7.3 billion, net of intercompany sales, came from our HD Supply segment and $2.0 billion came from our Retail segment.

Net Sales for our Retail segment were $79.0 billion for fiscal 2006, a 2.6% increase over fiscal 2005. Fiscal 2006 Retail segment Net Sales growth was primarily driven by sales from new stores. Retail comparable store sales decreased 2.8% for fiscal 2006 compared to an increase of 3.1% for fiscal 2005. The decline in retail comparable store sales was driven by a 4.6% decline in comparable store customer transactions offset in part by a 1.6% increase in average ticket. Our average ticket increased to $58.90 for fiscal 2006 and increased in 8 of 10 selling departments. The decrease in retail comparable store sales for fiscal 2006 was due to the significant slowdown in the U.S. retail home improvement market as well as difficult year-over-year comparisons due to sales arising from hurricane activity in fiscal 2005. Both Canada and Mexico, however, experienced positive retail comparable store sales for fiscal 2006. Additionally, our retail comparable store sales results reflect in part the impact of cannibalization. In order to meet our customer service objectives, we strategically open stores near market areas served by existing stores ("cannibalize") to enhance service levels, gain incremental sales and increase market penetration. Our new stores cannibalized approximately 13.5% of our existing stores during fiscal 2006, which had a negative impact to retail comparable store sales of approximately 1.9%.

Despite the difficult U.S. retail home improvement market, we continued to expand our retail services revenue, which increased 8.3% to $3.8 billion for fiscal 2006 from $3.5 billion for fiscal 2005. The growth in retail services revenue was driven by strength in a number of areas including countertops, exterior patios, solar, windows and HVAC. Our retail services programs focus primarily on providing products and services to our do-it-for-me customers. Our services revenue is expected to benefit from the growing percentage of aging "baby-boomers" as they rely more heavily on installation services.

Net Sales for our HD Supply segment for fiscal 2006 were $12.1 billion, an increase of 162% over fiscal 2005. The increase was primarily a result of recent acquisitions. Organic Net Sales growth for the HD Supply segment was 5.6% in fiscal 2006, which includes the impact of commodity price inflation and market share gains.

We believe that our sales performance has been, and could continue to be, negatively impacted by the level of competition that we encounter in various markets. Due to the highly-fragmented U.S. home improvement and professional supply industry, in which we estimate our market share is approximately 10%, measuring the impact on our sales by our competitors is difficult.

Gross Profit

Total Gross Profit increased 9.0% to $29.8 billion for fiscal 2006 from $27.3 billion for fiscal 2005. Gross Profit as a percent of Net Sales decreased 73 basis points to 32.8% for fiscal 2006 compared to 33.5% for fiscal 2005. The decline in total Gross Profit as a percent of Net Sales was primarily due to a higher penetration of the lower margin HD Supply segment. In fiscal 2006, 65 basis points of the total Gross Profit decline was a result of a higher penetration of HD Supply businesses as well as a drop in HD Supply's Gross Profit rate due to a change in the mix of businesses owned.

Operating Expenses

Operating Expenses increased 12.0% to $20.1 billion for fiscal 2006 from $18.0 billion for fiscal 2005. Operating Expenses as a percent of Net Sales were 22.1% for fiscal 2006 compared to 22.0% for fiscal 2005.

Selling, General and Administrative Expenses ("SG&A") increased 11.3% to $18.3 billion for fiscal 2006 from $16.5 billion for fiscal 2005. As a percent of Net Sales, SG&A was 20.2% for fiscal 2006 and fiscal 2005. The increase in SG&A during fiscal 2006 was due to added associate labor hours on the floor of our stores, increased spending on store maintenance programs and the expansion of merchandise display resets. This increase was partially offset by reduced self-insurance costs as we continue to realize benefits from safety programs and other initiatives. Fiscal 2006 SG&A also reflects benefits from our private label credit card, which carries a lower discount rate than other forms of credit, like bank cards. Through our private label credit card we offer no interest/no payment programs. The cost of deferred interest associated with these programs is included in Cost of Sales. We believe these programs deliver long-term benefits, including higher average ticket and customer loyalty. For fiscal 2006, the penetration of our private label credit sales was 28.0% compared to 25.6% for fiscal 2005.

Also impacting our SG&A in fiscal 2006 is expense associated with executive severance of $129 million and the adoption of Statement of Financial Accounting Standards ("SFAS") No. 123(R), "Share-Based Payment" ("SFAS 123(R)"), whereby we recorded approximately $40 million of stock compensation expense related to the continued vesting of options granted prior to fiscal 2003. Partially offsetting the increase in SG&A was $91 million of impairment charges and expense related to lease obligations associated with the closing of 20 EXPO stores in fiscal 2005.

Depreciation and Amortization increased 19.7% to $1.8 billion for fiscal 2006 from $1.5 billion for fiscal 2005. Depreciation and Amortization as a percent of Net Sales was 1.9% for fiscal 2006 and 1.8% for fiscal 2005. The increase as a percent of Net Sales was primarily due to the amortization of intangible assets acquired as part of our recent acquisitions and the depreciation of our investments in store modernization and technology.

Interest, net

In fiscal 2006, we recognized $365 million of net Interest Expense compared to $81 million in fiscal 2005. Net Interest Expense as a percent of Net Sales was 0.4% for fiscal 2006 compared to 0.1% for fiscal 2005. The increase was primarily due to additional interest incurred related to the March 2006 issuance of $1.0 billion of 5.20% Senior Notes and $3.0 billion of 5.40% Senior Notes and the December 2006 issuance of $750 million of floating rate Senior Notes, $1.25 billion of 5.25% Senior Notes and $3.0 billion of 5.875% Senior Notes.

Provision for Income Taxes

Our combined federal, state and foreign effective income tax rate increased to 38.1% for fiscal 2006 from 37.1% for fiscal 2005. The increase in our effective income tax rate for fiscal 2006 was primarily due to the impact of a retroactive tax assessment from the Canadian province of Quebec. During the second quarter of fiscal 2006, the Quebec National Assembly passed legislation that retroactively changed certain tax laws that subjected us to additional tax and interest. As a result, we received an assessment from Quebec for $57 million in retroactive tax and $12 million in related interest for the 2002 through 2005 taxable years.

Diluted Earnings per Share

Diluted Earnings per Share were $2.79 for fiscal 2006 and $2.72 for fiscal 2005. Diluted Earnings per Share were favorably impacted in both fiscal 2006 and fiscal 2005 by the repurchase of shares of our common stock under our $17.5 billion repurchase authorization. Since the inception of the program in 2002, we have repurchased 451 million shares of our common stock for a total of $16.4 billion, including $5 billion through accelerated share repurchases in fiscal 2006. As of January 28, 2007, we had $1.1 billion remaining under our authorized share repurchase program.

Fiscal 2005 Compared to Fiscal Year Ended January 30, 2005 ("fiscal 2004")

Net Sales

Net Sales for fiscal 2005 increased 11.5% to $81.5 billion from $73.1 billion for fiscal 2004. Fiscal 2005 Net Sales growth was driven by an increase in retail comparable store sales of 3.1%, sales from new stores opened during fiscal 2005 and fiscal 2004 and sales from our newly acquired businesses within HD Supply.

The increase in retail comparable store sales in fiscal 2005 reflects a number of factors. Our average ticket, which increased 5.6% to $57.98, increased in all selling departments and our retail comparable store sales growth in fiscal 2005 was positive in 9 of 10 selling departments. Building materials had the strongest retail comparable store sales increase through sales growth of gypsum, roofing, concrete and insulation, due in part to the impact of one of the most destructive hurricane seasons in modern U.S. history. We experienced strong retail comparable store sales growth in kitchen and bath driven by continued growth in appliances and kitchen installations. We also experienced strong retail comparable store sales in our Pro categories, including plumbing, electrical and hardware in fiscal 2005. The impact of cannibalization partially offset our fiscal 2005 retail comparable store sales growth. As of the end of fiscal 2005, certain new stores cannibalized approximately 20% of our existing stores and we estimate that store cannibalization reduced fiscal 2005 retail comparable store sales by approximately 1.8%.

The growth in Net Sales for fiscal 2005 also reflects growth in services revenue, which increased 16.6% to $3.5 billion for fiscal 2005 from $3.0 billion for fiscal 2004. The growth in services revenue was driven by strength in a number of areas including countertops, roofing, kitchens, windows and HVAC.

Gross Profit

Gross Profit increased 11.8% to $27.3 billion for fiscal 2005 from $24.4 billion for fiscal 2004. Gross Profit as a percent of Net Sales increased 10 basis points to 33.5% for fiscal 2005, the highest annual rate in our Company's history. Our gross profit margin was impacted by a number of factors during the year including a change in the mix of merchandise sold, markdowns taken in connection with our decision to close 20 EXPO stores, the increasing penetration of our HD Supply business and the cost of our deferred interest programs. For fiscal 2005, the penetration of our private label credit sales was 25.6% compared to 24.1% for fiscal 2004.

Operating Expenses

Operating Expenses increased 8.8% to $18.0 billion for fiscal 2005 from $16.5 billion for fiscal 2004. Operating Expenses as a percent of Net Sales were 22.0% for fiscal 2005 compared to 22.6% for fiscal 2004.

SG&A increased 8.1% to $16.5 billion for fiscal 2005 from $15.3 billion for fiscal 2004. As a percent of Net Sales, SG&A was 20.2% for fiscal 2005 compared to 20.9% for fiscal 2004. The reduction of SG&A as a percent of Net Sales for fiscal 2005 was primarily a result of continued focus on cost take-out initiatives and driving productivity gains throughout the Company. We also continue to see benefits from our private label credit card, which carries a lower discount rate than other forms of credit, like bank cards. In fiscal 2005, we recorded $52 million of income related to gift card breakage as a reduction of SG&A. Fiscal 2005 was the first year in which we recognized gift card breakage, and therefore, the amount recognized in fiscal 2005 includes the breakage income related to gift cards sold since the inception of our gift card program. Finally, for fiscal 2005, we recorded $91 million of impairment charges and expense related to lease obligations in connection with our decision to close 20 EXPO stores.

Depreciation and Amortization increased 17.9% to $1.5 billion for fiscal 2005 from $1.2 billion for fiscal 2004. Depreciation and Amortization as a percent of Net Sales was 1.8% for fiscal 2005 and 1.7% for fiscal 2004. The increase as a percent of Net Sales was primarily due to our investments in store modernization and technology.

Interest, net

In fiscal 2005, we recognized $81 million of net Interest Expense compared to $14 million in fiscal 2004. Net Interest Expense as a percent of Net Sales was 0.1% for fiscal 2005 and less than 0.1% for fiscal 2004. Interest Expense increased to $143 million for fiscal 2005 from $70 million for fiscal 2004 primarily due to additional interest incurred related to the August 2005 $1.0 billion issuance of 4.625% Senior Notes and the September 2004 $1.0 billion issuance of 3.75% Senior Notes. Interest and Investment Income increased 10.7% to $62 million for fiscal 2005 from $56 million for fiscal 2004 due primarily to a higher interest rate environment.

Provision for Income Taxes

Our combined federal and state effective income tax rate increased to 37.1% for fiscal 2005 from 36.8% for fiscal 2004. The majority of the increase in our effective income tax rate was due to an increase in the state effective tax rate in fiscal 2005.

Diluted Earnings per Share

Diluted Earnings per Share were $2.72 and $2.26 for fiscal 2005 and fiscal 2004, respectively. Diluted Earnings per Share were favorably impacted in both fiscal 2005 and fiscal 2004 as a result of the repurchase of shares of our common stock.

Liquidity and Capital Resources

Cash flow generated from operations provides a significant source of liquidity. For fiscal 2006, Net Cash Provided by Operating Activities was $7.7 billion as compared to $6.6 billion for fiscal 2005. The increase was primarily a result of more productive working capital in fiscal 2006.

Net Cash Used in Investing Activities increased to $7.6 billion for fiscal 2006 from $4.6 billion for fiscal 2005. This increase was primarily the result of an increase in Payments for Businesses Acquired of $1.7 billion as well as a decrease in net Proceeds from Sales and Maturities of Investments of $1.7 billion, partially offset by a $339 million decrease in Capital Expenditures. We paid $4.3 billion to complete 15 acquisitions in fiscal 2006, including Hughes Supply. Our fiscal 2006 acquisitions resulted in increases in Receivables, Merchandise Inventories, Goodwill, Other Assets and Accounts Payable in the Consolidated Balance Sheet as of January 28, 2007. See Note 11 to our "Notes to Consolidated Financial Statements" included in Item 8 of this report for further discussion.

Additionally in fiscal 2006, we spent $3.5 billion on Capital Expenditures, allocated as follows: 64% for new stores, 11% for store modernization, 6% for technology and 19% for other initiatives. In fiscal 2006, we added 125 new stores, including 12 stores in China through our acquisition of The Home Way, and 10 relocations.

Net Cash Used in Financing Activities for fiscal 2006 was $203 million compared with $1.7 billion for fiscal 2005. The decrease in Net Cash Used in Financing Activities was primarily due to net proceeds of $7.6 billion from the issuance of additional long-term debt, partially offset by a net increase of $4.2 billion in Repurchases of Common Stock and Cash Dividends Paid to Stockholders.

In February 2006, May 2006 and August 2006, our Board of Directors authorized an additional $1.0 billion, $2.0 billion and $3.5 billion, respectively, in our share repurchase program, bringing the total authorization by our Board of Directors since inception of the program in 2002 to $17.5 billion as of January 28, 2007. Pursuant to this authorization, we have repurchased approximately 451 million shares of our common stock for a total of $16.4 billion as of January 28, 2007. During fiscal 2006, we repurchased approximately 174 million shares of our common stock for $6.7 billion and during fiscal 2005 we repurchased approximately 76 million shares of our common stock for $3.0 billion. As of January 28, 2007, approximately $1.1 billion remained under our share repurchase program. During fiscal 2006, we also increased dividends paid by 62.8% to $1.4 billion from $857 million in fiscal 2005.

We have a commercial paper program that allows for borrowings up to $2.5 billion. In connection with the program, we have a back-up credit facility with a consortium of banks for borrowings up to $2.0 billion. As of January 28, 2007, there were no borrowings outstanding under the commercial paper program or the credit facility. The credit facility, which expires in December 2010, contains various restrictions, none of which is expected to impact our liquidity or capital resources.

We use capital and operating leases to finance a portion of our real estate, including our stores, distribution centers, HD Supply locations and store support centers. The net present value of capital lease obligations is reflected in our Consolidated Balance Sheets in Long-Term Debt. In accordance with generally accepted accounting principles, the operating leases are not reflected in our Consolidated Balance Sheets. As of the end of fiscal 2006, our long-term debt-to-equity ratio was 46.5% compared to 9.9% at the end of fiscal 2005. This increase reflects the net increase in Long-Term Debt as a result of the issuance of Senior Notes in March and December of fiscal 2006.

As of January 28, 2007, we had $614 million in Cash and Short-Term Investments. We believe that our current cash position and cash flow generated from operations should be sufficient to enable us to complete our capital expenditure programs and any required long-term debt payments through the next several fiscal years. In addition, we have funds available from the $2.5 billion commercial paper program and the ability to obtain alternative sources of financing for other requirements.

In March 2006, we entered into a forward starting interest rate swap agreement with a notional amount of $2.0 billion, accounted for as a cash flow hedge, to hedge interest rate fluctuations in anticipation of the issuance of the 5.40% Senior Notes due March 1, 2016. Upon issuance of the hedged debt, we settled our forward starting interest rate swap agreement and recorded a $12 million decrease, net of income taxes, to Accumulated Other Comprehensive Income, which will be amortized to interest expense over the life of the related debt.

In May 2006, we entered into a $2 billion accelerated share repurchase agreement with a financial institution pursuant to which we repurchased approximately 53 million shares of our common stock. Under the agreement, the financial institution purchased an equivalent number of shares of our common stock in the open market. The shares repurchased by us were subject to a future purchase price adjustment based upon the weighted average price of our common stock over an agreed period, subject to a specified collar. In August 2006, we settled the accelerated share repurchase. We elected settlement in cash and received $61 million from the financial institution, which was recorded as an offset to our cost of treasury stock.

In October 2006, we entered into a forward starting interest rate swap agreement with a notional amount of $1.0 billion, accounted for as a cash flow hedge, to hedge interest rate fluctuations in anticipation of the issuance of the 5.875% Senior Notes due December 16, 2036. Upon issuance of the hedged debt in December 2006, we settled our forward starting interest rate swap agreement and recorded an $11 million decrease, net of income taxes, to Accumulated Other Comprehensive Income, which will be amortized to interest expense over the life of the related debt.

In December 2006, we entered into a $3 billion accelerated share repurchase agreement with a financial institution pursuant to which we repurchased approximately 75 million shares of our common stock. Under the agreement, the financial institution purchased an equivalent number of shares of our common stock in the open market. The shares repurchased by us were subject to a future purchase price adjustment based upon the weighted average price of our common stock over an agreed period. In March 2007, we settled the accelerated share repurchase. We elected settlement in cash and received $36 million from the financial institution, which was recorded as an offset to our cost of treasury stock in fiscal 2007.

The following table summarizes our significant contractual obligations and commercial commitments as of January 28, 2007 (amounts in millions):

| Contractual Obligations[1] | Payments Due by Fiscal Year | | | | |
	Total	2007	2008-2009	2010-2011	Thereafter
Total Debt[2]	$19,358	$ 607	$3,224	$2,946	$12,581
Capital Lease Obligations[3]	1,323	78	157	160	928
Operating Leases	9,131	917	1,580	1,213	5,421
Subtotal	$29,812	$1,602	$4,961	$4,319	$18,930

| Commercial Commitments[4] | Amount of Commitment Expiration per Fiscal Year | | | | |
	Total	2007	2008-2009	2010-2011	Thereafter
Letters of Credit	$ 1,238	$1,230	$ 8	$ —	$ —
Purchase Obligations[5]	2,741	1,379	1,336	22	4
Guarantees	72	72	—	—	—
Subtotal	4,051	2,681	1,344	22	4
Total	$33,863	$4,283	$6,305	$4,341	$18,934

(1) *Contractual obligations include Long-Term Debt comprised primarily of $11 billion of Senior Notes further discussed in "Quantitative and Qualitative Disclosures about Market Risk" and future minimum lease payments under capital and operating leases used in the normal course of business.*

(2) *Excludes present value of capital lease obligations of $419 million. Includes $8.0 billion of interest payments and $69 million of unamortized discount.*

(3) *Includes $904 million of imputed interest.*

(4) *Commercial commitments include letters of credit from certain business transactions, purchase obligations and commitments to purchase store assets. We issue letters of credit for insurance programs, purchases of import merchandise inventories and construction contracts. Our purchase obligations consist of commitments for both merchandise and services.*

(5) *Purchase obligations include all legally binding contracts such as firm commitments for inventory purchases, utility purchases, capital expenditures, software acquisition and license commitments and legally binding service contracts. Purchase orders that are not binding agreements are excluded from the table above. Additionally, we have included a commitment to purchase the underlying asset under an off-balance sheet lease related to certain stores for $282 million during 2008.*

Quantitative and Qualitative Disclosures about Market Risk

Our exposure to market risk results primarily from fluctuations in interest rates. Although we have international operating entities, our exposure to foreign currency rate fluctuations is not significant to our financial condition and results of operations. Our primary objective for entering into derivative instruments is to manage our exposure to interest rates, as well as to maintain an appropriate mix of fixed and variable rate debt.

As of January 28, 2007 we had, net of discounts, $10.9 billion of Senior Notes outstanding. The market values of the publicly traded Senior Notes as of January 28, 2007, were approximately $10.9 billion.

Impact of Inflation, Deflation and Changing Prices

We have experienced inflation and deflation related to our purchase of certain commodity products. During fiscal 2006, lumber prices decreased our comparable store sales by approximately 43 basis points. We do not believe that changing prices for commodities have had a material effect on our Net Sales or results of operations. Although we cannot precisely determine the overall effect of inflation and deflation on operations, we do not believe inflation and deflation have had a material effect on our results of operations.

Critical Accounting Policies

Our significant accounting policies are disclosed in Note 1 of our Consolidated Financial Statements. The following discussion addresses our most critical accounting policies, which are those that are both important to the portrayal of our financial condition and results of operations and that require significant judgment or use of complex estimates.

Revenue Recognition

We recognize revenue, net of estimated returns, at the time the customer takes possession of the merchandise or receives services. We estimate the liability for sales returns based on our historical return levels. We believe that our estimate for sales returns is an accurate reflection of future returns. We have never recorded a significant adjustment to our estimated liability for sales returns. However, if these estimates are significantly below the actual amounts, our sales could be adversely impacted. When we receive payment from customers before the customer has taken possession of the merchandise or the service has been performed, the amount received is recorded as Deferred Revenue in the accompanying Consolidated Balance Sheets until the sale or service is complete.

Merchandise Inventories

Our Merchandise Inventories are stated at the lower of cost (first-in, first-out) or market, with approximately 80% valued under the retail inventory method and the remainder under the cost method. Retailers like The Home Depot, with many different types of merchandise at low unit cost and a large number of transactions, frequently use the retail inventory method. Under the retail inventory method, Merchandise Inventories are stated at cost, which is determined by applying a cost-to-retail ratio to the ending retail value of inventories. As our inventory retail value is adjusted regularly to reflect market conditions, our inventory valued under the retail method approximates the lower of cost or market. We evaluate our inventory valued under the cost method at the end of each quarter to ensure that it is carried at the lower of cost or market. The valuation allowance for Merchandise Inventories valued under the cost method was not material to the Consolidated Financial Statements of the Company as of the end of fiscal 2006 and fiscal 2005.

Independent physical inventory counts or cycle counts are taken on a regular basis in each store, distribution center and HD Supply location to ensure that amounts reflected in the accompanying Consolidated Financial Statements for Merchandise Inventories are properly stated. During the period between physical inventory counts in our stores, we accrue for estimated losses related to shrink on a store-by-store basis. Shrink (or in the case of excess inventory, "swell") is the difference between the recorded amount of inventory and the physical inventory. Shrink may occur due to theft, loss, inaccurate records for the receipt of inventory or deterioration of goods, among other things. We estimate shrink as a percent of Net Sales using the average shrink results from the previous two physical inventories. The estimates are evaluated quarterly and adjusted based on recent shrink results and current trends in the business.

Self-Insurance

We are self-insured for certain losses related to general liability, product liability, automobile, workers' compensation and medical claims. Our liability represents an estimate of the ultimate cost of claims incurred as of the balance sheet date. The estimated liability is not discounted and is established based upon analysis of historical data and actuarial estimates, and is reviewed by management and third-party actuaries on a quarterly basis to ensure that the liability is appropriate. While we believe these estimates are reasonable based on the information currently available, if actual trends, including the severity or frequency of claims, medical cost inflation, or fluctuations in premiums, differ from our estimates, our results of operations could be impacted.

Vendor Allowances

Vendor allowances primarily consist of volume rebates that are earned as a result of attaining certain purchase levels and advertising co-op allowances for the promotion of vendors' products that are typically based on guaranteed minimum amounts with additional amounts being earned for attaining certain purchase levels. These vendor allowances are accrued as earned, with those allowances received as a result of attaining certain purchase levels accrued over the incentive period based on estimates of purchases. We believe that our estimate of vendor allowances earned based on expected volume of purchases over the incentive period is an accurate reflection of the ultimate allowance to be received from our vendors.

Volume rebates and advertising co-op allowances earned are initially recorded as a reduction in Merchandise Inventories and a subsequent reduction in Cost of Sales when the related product is sold. Certain advertising co-op allowances that are reimbursements of specific, incremental and identifiable costs incurred to promote vendors' products are recorded as an offset against advertising expense.

Recent Accounting Pronouncements

In September 2006, the Securities and Exchange Commission ("SEC") issued Staff Accounting Bulletin No. 108, "Considering the Effects of Prior Year Misstatements when Quantifying Misstatements in Current Year Financial Statements" ("SAB 108"). SAB 108 addresses the process of quantifying prior year financial statement misstatements and their impact on current year financial statements. The provisions of SAB 108 allow companies to report the cumulative effect of correcting immaterial prior year misstatements, based on the Company's historical method for evaluating misstatements, by adjusting the opening balance of retained earnings in the current year financial statements rather than amending previously filed reports. SAB 108 also requires disclosure of the nature and amount of each individual error being corrected, how the event arose and the fact that the errors are considered immaterial to the prior year financial statements. SAB 108 is effective for fiscal years ending after November 15, 2006, and therefore was effective for The Home Depot in fiscal 2006. See Note 2 to our "Notes to Consolidated Financial Statements" included in Item 8 of this report for further discussion.

In July 2006, the Financial Accounting Standards Board ("FASB") issued FASB Interpretation No. 48, "Accounting for Uncertainty in Income Taxes – an Interpretation of FASB Statement No. 109" ("FIN 48"). FIN 48 clarifies the accounting for uncertainty in income tax reporting by prescribing a recognition threshold and measurement attribute for the financial statement recognition and measurement of a tax position taken or expected to be taken in a tax return. FIN 48 requires that companies recognize tax benefits in their financial statements for a tax position only if that position is more likely than not of being sustained on audit, based on the technical merits of the position. Additionally, FIN 48 provides guidance on de-recognition, classification, interest and penalties, accounting in interim periods, disclosure and transition. FIN 48 becomes effective for fiscal years beginning after December 15, 2006, and will therefore be effective for The Home Depot in fiscal 2007. The cumulative impact of adopting FIN 48 in fiscal 2007 is not expected to have a material impact on the financial condition of the Company.

Item 7A. Quantitative and Qualitative Disclosures About Market Risk.

The information required by this item is incorporated by reference to Item 7. "Management's Discussion and Analysis of Financial Conditions and Results of Operations" of this report.

Item 8. Financial Statements and Supplementary Data.

Management's Responsibility for Financial Statements

The financial statements presented in this Annual Report have been prepared with integrity and objectivity and are the responsibility of the management of The Home Depot, Inc. These financial statements have been prepared in conformity with U.S. generally accepted accounting principles and properly reflect certain estimates and judgments based upon the best available information.

The financial statements of the Company have been audited by KPMG LLP, an independent registered public accounting firm. Their accompanying report is based upon an audit conducted in accordance with the standards of the Public Company Accounting Oversight Board (United States).

The Audit Committee of the Board of Directors, consisting solely of outside directors, meets five times a year with the independent registered public accounting firm, the internal auditors and representatives of management to discuss auditing and financial reporting matters. In addition, a telephonic meeting is held prior to each quarterly earnings release. The Audit Committee retains the independent registered public accounting firm and regularly reviews the internal accounting controls, the activities of the independent registered public accounting firm and internal auditors and the financial condition of the Company. Both the Company's independent registered pubic accounting firm and the internal auditors have free access to the Audit Committee.

Management's Report on Internal Control over Financial Reporting

Our management is responsible for establishing and maintaining adequate internal control over financial reporting, as such term is defined in Rule 13a-15(f) promulgated under the Securities Exchange Act of 1934, as amended. Under the supervision and with the participation of our management, including our principal executive officer and principal financial officer, we conducted an evaluation of the effectiveness of our internal control over financial reporting based on the framework in *Internal Control – Integrated Framework* issued by the Committee of Sponsoring Organizations of the Treadway Commission (COSO). Based on our evaluation, our management concluded that our internal control over financial reporting was effective as of January 28, 2007 in providing reasonable assurance regarding reliability of financial reporting and the preparation of financial statements for external purposes in accordance with generally accepted accounting principles. Our management's assessment of the effectiveness of our internal control over financial reporting as of January 28, 2007 has been audited by KPMG LLP, an independent registered public accounting firm, as stated in its report which is included herein.

/s/ FRANCIS S. BLAKE

Francis S. Blake
Chairman &
Chief Executive Officer

/s/ CAROL B. TOMÉ

Carol B. Tomé
Chief Financial Officer &
Executive Vice President –
Corporate Services

Report of Independent Registered Public Accounting Firm

The Board of Directors and Stockholders
The Home Depot, Inc.:

We have audited management's assessment, included in the accompanying Management's Report on Internal Control Over Financial Reporting, that The Home Depot, Inc. and subsidiaries maintained effective internal control over financial reporting as of January 28, 2007, based on criteria established in *Internal Control – Integrated Framework* issued by the Committee of Sponsoring Organizations of the Treadway Commission (COSO). The Company's management is responsible for maintaining effective internal control over financial reporting and for its assessment of the effectiveness of internal control over financial reporting. Our responsibility is to express an opinion on management's assessment and an opinion on the effectiveness of the Company's internal control over financial reporting based on our audit.

We conducted our audit in accordance with the standards of the Public Company Accounting Oversight Board (United States). Those standards require that we plan and perform the audit to obtain reasonable assurance about whether effective internal control over financial reporting was maintained in all material respects. Our audit included obtaining an understanding of internal control over financial reporting, evaluating management's assessment, testing and evaluating the design and operating effectiveness of internal control, and performing such other procedures as we considered necessary in the circumstances. We believe that our audit provides a reasonable basis for our opinion.

A company's internal control over financial reporting is a process designed to provide reasonable assurance regarding the reliability of financial reporting and the preparation of financial statements for external purposes in accordance with generally accepted accounting principles. A company's internal control over financial reporting includes those policies and procedures that (1) pertain to the maintenance of records that, in reasonable detail, accurately and fairly reflect the transactions and dispositions of the assets of the company; (2) provide reasonable assurance that transactions are recorded as necessary to permit preparation of financial statements in accordance with generally accepted accounting principles, and that receipts and expenditures of the company are being made only in accordance with authorizations of management and directors of the company; and (3) provide reasonable assurance regarding prevention or timely detection of unauthorized acquisition, use, or disposition of the company's assets that could have a material effect on the financial statements.

Because of its inherent limitations, internal control over financial reporting may not prevent or detect misstatements. Also, projections of any evaluation of effectiveness to future periods are subject to the risk that controls may become inadequate because of changes in conditions, or that the degree of compliance with the policies or procedures may deteriorate.

In our opinion, management's assessment that The Home Depot, Inc. and subsidiaries maintained effective internal control over financial reporting as of January 28, 2007, is fairly stated, in all material respects, based on criteria established in *Internal Control – Integrated Framework* issued by the Committee of Sponsoring Organizations of the Treadway Commission (COSO). Also, in our opinion, The Home Depot, Inc. and subsidiaries maintained, in all material respects, effective internal control over financial reporting as of January 28, 2007, based on criteria established in *Internal Control – Integrated Framework* issued by the Committee of Sponsoring Organizations of the Treadway Commission (COSO).

We also have audited, in accordance with the standards of the Public Company Accounting Oversight Board (United States), the Consolidated Balance Sheets of The Home Depot, Inc. and subsidiaries as of January 28, 2007 and January 29, 2006, and the related Consolidated Statements of Earnings, Stockholders' Equity and Comprehensive Income, and Cash Flows for each of the fiscal years in the three-year period ended January 28, 2007, and our report dated March 21, 2007 expressed an unqualified opinion on those consolidated financial statements. Our report refers to the Company's adoption of Securities and Exchange Commission Staff Accounting Bulletin No. 108, *Considering the Effects of Prior Year Misstatements when Quantifying Misstatements in the Current Year Financial Statements*, effective January 30, 2006, the beginning of the fiscal year ended January 28, 2007.

/s/ KPMG LLP

Atlanta, Georgia
March 21, 2007

Report of Independent Registered Public Accounting Firm

The Board of Directors and Stockholders
The Home Depot, Inc.:

We have audited the accompanying Consolidated Balance Sheets of The Home Depot, Inc. and subsidiaries as of January 28, 2007 and January 29, 2006, and the related Consolidated Statements of Earnings, Stockholders' Equity and Comprehensive Income, and Cash Flows for each of the fiscal years in the three-year period ended January 28, 2007. These Consolidated Financial Statements are the responsibility of the Company's management. Our responsibility is to express an opinion on these Consolidated Financial Statements based on our audits.

We conducted our audits in accordance with the standards of the Public Company Accounting Oversight Board (United States). Those standards require that we plan and perform the audit to obtain reasonable assurance about whether the financial statements are free of material misstatement. An audit includes examining, on a test basis, evidence supporting the amounts and disclosures in the financial statements. An audit also includes assessing the accounting principles used and significant estimates made by management, as well as evaluating the overall financial statement presentation. We believe that our audits provide a reasonable basis for our opinion.

In our opinion, the Consolidated Financial Statements referred to above present fairly, in all material respects, the financial position of The Home Depot, Inc. and subsidiaries as of January 28, 2007 and January 29, 2006, and the results of their operations and their cash flows for each of the fiscal years in the three-year period ended January 28, 2007, in conformity with U.S. generally accepted accounting principles.

As discussed in Note 2 to the consolidated financial statements, effective January 30, 2006, the beginning of the fiscal year ended January 28, 2007, the Company adopted Securities and Exchange Commission Staff Accounting Bulletin No. 108, *Considering the Effects of Prior Year Misstatements when Quantifying Misstatements in the Current Year Financial Statements*.

We also have audited, in accordance with the standards of the Public Company Accounting Oversight Board (United States), the effectiveness of The Home Depot, Inc.'s internal control over financial reporting as of January 28, 2007, based on criteria established in *Internal Control – Integrated Framework* issued by the Committee of Sponsoring Organizations of the Treadway Commission (COSO), and our report dated March 21, 2007 expressed an unqualified opinion on management's assessment of, and the effective operation of, internal control over financial reporting.

/s/ KPMG LLP

Atlanta, Georgia
March 21, 2007

THE HOME DEPOT, INC. AND SUBSIDIARIES
CONSOLIDATED STATEMENTS OF EARNINGS

	Fiscal Year Ended[1]		
amounts in millions, except per share data	January 28, 2007	January 29, 2006	January 30, 2005
NET SALES	$90,837	$81,511	$73,094
Cost of Sales	61,054	54,191	48,664
GROSS PROFIT	29,783	27,320	24,430
Operating Expenses:			
Selling, General and Administrative	18,348	16,485	15,256
Depreciation and Amortization	1,762	1,472	1,248
Total Operating Expenses	20,110	17,957	16,504
OPERATING INCOME	9,673	9,363	7,926
Interest Income (Expense):			
Interest and Investment Income	27	62	56
Interest Expense	(392)	(143)	(70)
Interest, net	(365)	(81)	(14)
EARNINGS BEFORE PROVISION FOR INCOME TAXES	9,308	9,282	7,912
Provision for Income Taxes	3,547	3,444	2,911
NET EARNINGS	$ 5,761	$ 5,838	$ 5,001
Weighted Average Common Shares	2,054	2,138	2,207
BASIC EARNINGS PER SHARE	$ 2.80	$ 2.73	$ 2.27
Diluted Weighted Average Common Shares	2,062	2,147	2,216
DILUTED EARNINGS PER SHARE	$ 2.79	$ 2.72	$ 2.26

(1) Fiscal years ended January 28, 2007, January 29, 2006 and January 30, 2005 include 52 weeks.

See accompanying Notes to Consolidated Financial Statements.

THE HOME DEPOT, INC. AND SUBSIDIARIES
CONSOLIDATED BALANCE SHEETS

amounts in millions, except per share data	January 28, 2007	January 29, 2006
ASSETS		
Current Assets:		
Cash and Cash Equivalents	$ 600	$ 793
Short-Term Investments	14	14
Receivables, net	3,223	2,396
Merchandise Inventories	12,822	11,401
Other Current Assets	1,341	665
Total Current Assets	18,000	15,269
Property and Equipment, at cost:		
Land	8,355	7,924
Buildings	15,215	14,056
Furniture, Fixtures and Equipment	7,799	7,073
Leasehold Improvements	1,391	1,207
Construction in Progress	1,123	843
Capital Leases	475	427
	34,358	31,530
Less Accumulated Depreciation and Amortization	7,753	6,629
Net Property and Equipment	26,605	24,901
Notes Receivable	343	348
Goodwill	6,314	3,286
Other Assets	1,001	601
Total Assets	$52,263	$44,405
LIABILITIES AND STOCKHOLDERS' EQUITY		
Current Liabilities:		
Short-Term Debt	$ —	$ 900
Accounts Payable	7,356	6,032
Accrued Salaries and Related Expenses	1,295	1,068
Sales Taxes Payable	475	488
Deferred Revenue	1,634	1,757
Income Taxes Payable	217	388
Current Installments of Long-Term Debt	18	513
Other Accrued Expenses	1,936	1,560
Total Current Liabilities	12,931	12,706
Long-Term Debt, excluding current installments	11,643	2,672
Other Long-Term Liabilities	1,243	1,172
Deferred Income Taxes	1,416	946
STOCKHOLDERS' EQUITY		
Common Stock, par value $0.05; authorized: 10,000 shares; issued 2,421 shares at January 28, 2007 and 2,401 shares at January 29, 2006; outstanding 1,970 shares at January 28, 2007 and 2,124 shares at January 29, 2006	121	120
Paid-In Capital	7,930	7,149
Retained Earnings	33,052	28,943
Accumulated Other Comprehensive Income	310	409
Treasury Stock, at cost, 451 shares at January 28, 2007 and 277 shares at January 29, 2006	(16,383)	(9,712)
Total Stockholders' Equity	25,030	26,909
Total Liabilities and Stockholders' Equity	$52,263	$44,405

See accompanying Notes to Consolidated Financial Statements.

THE HOME DEPOT, INC. AND SUBSIDIARIES
CONSOLIDATED STATEMENTS OF STOCKHOLDERS'
EQUITY AND COMPREHENSIVE INCOME

amounts in millions, except per share data	Common Stock Shares	Common Stock Amount	Paid-In Capital	Retained Earnings	Accumulated Other Comprehensive Income (Loss)	Treasury Stock Shares	Treasury Stock Amount	Stockholders' Equity	Total Comprehensive Income
BALANCE, FEBRUARY 1, 2004	**2,373**	**$119**	**$6,108**	**$19,680**	**$ 90**	**(116)**	**$ (3,590)**	**$22,407**	
Net Earnings	—	—	—	5,001	—	—	—	5,001	$5,001
Shares Issued Under Employee Stock Plans	12	—	286	—	—	—	—	286	
Tax Effect of Sale of Option Shares by Employees	—	—	26	—	—	—	—	26	
Translation Adjustments	—	—	—	—	137	—	—	137	137
Stock Options, Awards and Amortization of Restricted Stock	—	—	122	—	—	—	—	122	
Repurchase of Common Stock	—	—	—	—	—	(84)	(3,102)	(3,102)	
Cash Dividends ($0.325 per share)	—	—	—	(719)	—	—	—	(719)	
Comprehensive Income									$5,138
BALANCE, JANUARY 30, 2005	**2,385**	**$119**	**$6,542**	**$23,962**	**$227**	**(200)**	**$ (6,692)**	**$24,158**	
Net Earnings	—	—	—	5,838	—	—	—	5,838	$5,838
Shares Issued Under Employee Stock Plans	16	1	409	—	—	—	—	410	
Tax Effect of Sale of Option Shares by Employees	—	—	24	—	—	—	—	24	
Translation Adjustments	—	—	—	—	182	—	—	182	182
Stock Options, Awards and Amortization of Restricted Stock	—	—	174	—	—	—	—	174	
Repurchase of Common Stock	—	—	—	—	—	(77)	(3,020)	(3,020)	
Cash Dividends ($0.40 per share)	—	—	—	(857)	—	—	—	(857)	
Comprehensive Income									$6,020
BALANCE, JANUARY 29, 2006	**2,401**	**$120**	**$7,149**	**$28,943**	**$409**	**(277)**	**$ (9,712)**	**$26,909**	
Cumulative Effect of Adjustments Resulting from the Adoption of SAB 108, net of tax	—	—	201	(257)	—	—	—	(56)	
ADJUSTED BALANCE, JANUARY 29, 2006	**2,401**	**$120**	**$7,350**	**$28,686**	**$409**	**(277)**	**$ (9,712)**	**$26,853**	
Net Earnings	—	—	—	5,761	—	—	—	5,761	$5,761
Shares Issued Under Employee Stock Plans	20	1	351	—	—	—	—	352	
Tax Effect of Sale of Option Shares by Employees	—	—	18	—	—	—	—	18	
Translation Adjustments	—	—	—	—	(77)	—	—	(77)	(77)
Interest Rate Hedges	—	—	—	—	(22)	—	—	(22)	(22)
Stock Options, Awards and Amortization of Restricted Stock	—	—	296	—	—	—	—	296	
Repurchase of Common Stock	—	—	—	—	—	(174)	(6,671)	(6,671)	
Cash Dividends ($0.675 per share)	—	—	—	(1,395)	—	—	—	(1,395)	
Other	—	—	(85)	—	—	—	—	(85)	
Comprehensive Income									$5,662
BALANCE, JANUARY 28, 2007	**2,421**	**$121**	**$7,930**	**$33,052**	**$310**	**(451)**	**$(16,383)**	**$25,030**	

See accompanying Notes to Consolidated Financial Statements.

THE HOME DEPOT, INC. AND SUBSIDIARIES
CONSOLIDATED STATEMENTS OF CASH FLOWS

amounts in millions	Fiscal Year Ended[1]		
	January 28, 2007	January 29, 2006	January 30, 2005
CASH FLOWS FROM OPERATING ACTIVITIES:			
Net Earnings	$ 5,761	$ 5,838	$ 5,001
Reconciliation of Net Earnings to Net Cash Provided by Operating Activities:			
Depreciation and Amortization	1,886	1,579	1,319
Impairment Related to Disposition of EXPO Real Estate	—	78	—
Stock-Based Compensation Expense	297	175	125
Changes in Assets and Liabilities, net of the effects of acquisitions:			
Decrease (Increase) in Receivables, net	96	(358)	(266)
Increase in Merchandise Inventories	(563)	(971)	(849)
(Increase) Decrease in Other Current Assets	(225)	16	29
Increase in Accounts Payable and Accrued Liabilities	531	148	645
(Decrease) Increase in Deferred Revenue	(123)	209	263
(Decrease) Increase in Income Taxes Payable	(172)	175	2
Increase (Decrease) in Deferred Income Taxes	46	(609)	319
(Decrease) Increase in Other Long-Term Liabilities	(51)	151	119
Other	178	189	(75)
Net Cash Provided by Operating Activities	7,661	6,620	6,632
CASH FLOWS FROM INVESTING ACTIVITIES:			
Capital Expenditures, net of $49, $51 and $38 of non-cash capital expenditures in fiscal 2006, 2005 and 2004, respectively	(3,542)	(3,881)	(3,948)
Payments for Businesses Acquired, net	(4,268)	(2,546)	(727)
Proceeds from Sales of Property and Equipment	138	164	96
Purchases of Investments	(5,409)	(18,230)	(25,890)
Proceeds from Sales and Maturities of Investments	5,434	19,907	25,990
Net Cash Used in Investing Activities	(7,647)	(4,586)	(4,479)
CASH FLOWS FROM FINANCING ACTIVITIES:			
(Repayments of) Proceeds from Short-Term Borrowings, net	(900)	900	—
Proceeds from Long-Term Borrowings, net of discount	8,935	995	995
Repayments of Long-Term Debt	(509)	(24)	(510)
Repurchases of Common Stock	(6,684)	(3,040)	(3,106)
Proceeds from Sale of Common Stock	381	414	285
Cash Dividends Paid to Stockholders	(1,395)	(857)	(719)
Other Financing Activities	(31)	(136)	272
Net Cash Used in Financing Activities	(203)	(1,748)	(2,783)
(Decrease) Increase in Cash and Cash Equivalents	(189)	286	(630)
Effect of Exchange Rate Changes on Cash and Cash Equivalents	(4)	1	33
Cash and Cash Equivalents at Beginning of Year	793	506	1,103
Cash and Cash Equivalents at End of Year	$ 600	$ 793	$ 506
SUPPLEMENTAL DISCLOSURE OF CASH PAYMENTS MADE FOR:			
Interest, net of interest capitalized	$ 270	$ 114	$ 78
Income Taxes	$ 3,963	$ 3,860	$ 2,793

(1) *Fiscal years ended January 28, 2007, January 29, 2006 and January 30, 2005 include 52 weeks.*

See accompanying Notes to Consolidated Financial Statements.

NOTES TO CONSOLIDATED FINANCIAL STATEMENTS

1. SUMMARY OF SIGNIFICANT ACCOUNTING POLICIES

Business, Consolidation and Presentation

The Home Depot, Inc. and its subsidiaries (the "Company") operate The Home Depot stores, which are full-service, warehouse-style stores averaging approximately 105,000 square feet in size. The stores stock approximately 35,000 to 45,000 different kinds of building materials, home improvement supplies and lawn and garden products that are sold to do-it-yourself customers, do-it-for-me customers, home improvement contractors, tradespeople and building maintenance professionals. In addition, the Company operates EXPO Design Center stores ("EXPO"), which offer products and services primarily related to design and renovation projects, and The Home Depot Landscape Supply stores, which service landscape professionals and garden enthusiasts with lawn, landscape and garden products. At the end of fiscal 2006, the Company was operating 2,147 stores in total, which included 1,872 The Home Depot stores, 34 EXPO Design Center stores, 11 The Home Depot Landscape Supply stores and two The Home Depot Floor Stores in the United States, including the territories of Puerto Rico and the Virgin Islands ("U.S."), 155 The Home Depot stores in Canada, 61 The Home Depot stores in Mexico and 12 The Home Depot stores in China.

Additionally, HD Supply, through the Company's wholly-owned subsidiaries, distributes products and sells installation services primarily to business-to-business customers, including home builders, professional contractors, municipalities and maintenance professionals. HD Supply consists of four major platforms: 1) infrastructure, including waterworks and utilities; 2) construction, including construction supply, lumber and building materials, electrical, plumbing/HVAC and interiors; 3) maintenance, including facilities maintenance and industrial PVF; and 4) repair and remodel.

The Company operates its business in two reportable segments, Retail and HD Supply. See Note 12 for further information on the Company's segments. The Consolidated Financial Statements include the accounts of the Company and its wholly-owned subsidiaries. All significant intercompany transactions have been eliminated in consolidation.

Fiscal Year

The Company's fiscal year is a 52- or 53-week period ending on the Sunday nearest to January 31. Fiscal years ended January 28, 2007 ("fiscal 2006"), January 29, 2006 ("fiscal 2005") and January 30, 2005 ("fiscal 2004") include 52 weeks.

Use of Estimates

Management of the Company has made a number of estimates and assumptions relating to the reporting of assets and liabilities, the disclosure of contingent assets and liabilities, and reported amounts of revenues and expenses in preparing these financial statements in conformity with generally accepted accounting principles. Actual results could differ from these estimates.

Fair Value of Financial Instruments

The carrying amounts of Cash and Cash Equivalents, Receivables, Short-Term Debt and Accounts Payable approximate fair value due to the short-term maturities of these financial instruments. The fair value of the Company's investments is discussed under the caption "Short-Term Investments" in this Note 1. The fair value of the Company's Long-Term Debt is discussed in Note 4.

Cash Equivalents

The Company considers all highly liquid investments purchased with maturities of three months or less to be cash equivalents. The Company's Cash Equivalents are carried at fair market value and consist primarily of high-grade commercial paper, money market funds, U.S. government agency securities and tax-exempt notes and bonds.

Short-Term Investments

Short-Term Investments are recorded at fair value based on current market rates and are classified as available-for-sale. Changes in the fair value are included in Accumulated Other Comprehensive Income (Loss), net of applicable taxes, in the accompanying Consolidated Financial Statements. The Company periodically invests in auction rate securities, which are debt instruments with long-term scheduled maturities and periodic interest rate reset dates. The interest rates on these securities are typically reset to market prevailing rates every 35 days or less, and in all cases every 90 days or less. Due to the liquidity provided by the interest rate reset mechanism and the short-term nature of the Company's investment in these securities, they have been classified as current assets in the accompanying Consolidated Balance Sheets.

Accounts Receivable

The Company has an agreement with a third-party service provider who directly extends credit to customers and manages the Company's private label credit card program. In addition, certain subsidiaries of the Company extend credit directly to customers in the ordinary course of business. The receivables due from customers were $1.8 billion and $865 million as of January 28, 2007 and January 29, 2006, respectively. The Company's valuation reserve related to accounts receivable was not material to the Consolidated Financial Statements of the Company as of the end of fiscal 2006 and fiscal 2005.

Merchandise Inventories

The majority of the Company's Merchandise Inventories are stated at the lower of cost (first-in, first-out) or market, as determined by the retail inventory method. As the inventory retail value is adjusted regularly to reflect market conditions, the inventory valued using the retail method approximates the lower of cost or market. Certain subsidiaries, including retail operations in Mexico and China, and distribution centers record Merchandise Inventories at the lower of cost (first-in, first-out) or market, as determined by the cost method. These Merchandise Inventories represent approximately 20% of the total Merchandise Inventories balance. The Company evaluates the inventory valued using the cost method at the end of each quarter to ensure that it is carried at the lower of cost or market. The valuation allowance for Merchandise Inventories valued under the cost method was not material to the Consolidated Financial Statements of the Company as of the end of fiscal 2006 and fiscal 2005.

Independent physical inventory counts or cycle counts are taken on a regular basis in each store, distribution center and HD Supply location to ensure that amounts reflected in the accompanying Consolidated Financial Statements for Merchandise Inventories are properly stated. During the period between physical inventory counts in stores, the Company accrues for estimated losses related to shrink on a store-by-store basis based on historical shrink results and current trends in the business. Shrink (or in the case of excess inventory, "swell") is the difference between the recorded amount of inventory and the physical inventory. Shrink may occur due to theft, loss, inaccurate records for the receipt of inventory or deterioration of goods, among other things.

Income Taxes

The Company provides for federal, state and foreign income taxes currently payable, as well as for those deferred due to timing differences between reporting income and expenses for financial statement purposes versus tax purposes. Federal, state and foreign tax benefits are recorded as a reduction of income taxes. Deferred tax assets and liabilities are recognized for the future tax consequences attributable to temporary differences between the financial statement carrying amounts of existing assets and liabilities and their respective tax bases. Deferred tax assets and liabilities are measured using enacted income tax rates expected to apply to taxable income in the years in which those temporary differences are expected to be recovered or settled. The effect of a change in income tax rates is recognized as income or expense in the period that includes the enactment date.

The Company and its eligible subsidiaries file a consolidated U.S. federal income tax return. Non-U.S. subsidiaries and certain U.S. subsidiaries, which are consolidated for financial reporting purposes, are not eligible to be included in the Company's consolidated U.S. federal income tax return. Separate provisions for income taxes have been determined for these entities. The Company intends to reinvest the unremitted earnings of its non-U.S. subsidiaries and postpone their remittance indefinitely. Accordingly, no provision for U.S. income taxes for non-U.S. subsidiaries was recorded in the accompanying Consolidated Statements of Earnings.

Depreciation and Amortization

The Company's Buildings, Furniture, Fixtures and Equipment are depreciated using the straight-line method over the estimated useful lives of the assets. Leasehold Improvements are amortized using the straight-line method over the original term of the lease or the useful life of the improvement, whichever is shorter. The Company's Property and Equipment is depreciated using the following estimated useful lives:

	Life
Buildings	10-45 years
Furniture, Fixtures and Equipment	3-20 years
Leasehold Improvements	5-45 years

Capitalized Software Costs

The Company capitalizes certain costs related to the acquisition and development of software and amortizes these costs using the straight-line method over the estimated useful life of the software, which is three to six years. These costs are included in Furniture, Fixtures and Equipment in the accompanying Consolidated Balance Sheets. Certain development costs not meeting the criteria for capitalization are expensed as incurred.

Revenues

The Company recognizes revenue, net of estimated returns, at the time the customer takes possession of merchandise or receives services. The liability for sales returns is estimated based on historical return levels. When the Company receives payment from customers before the customer has taken possession of the merchandise or the service has been performed, the amount received is recorded as Deferred Revenue in the accompanying Consolidated Balance Sheets until the sale or service is complete. The Company also records Deferred Revenue for the sale of gift cards and recognizes this revenue upon the redemption of gift cards in Net Sales. Gift card breakage income is recognized based upon historical redemption patterns and represents the balance of gift cards for which the Company believes the likelihood of redemption by the customer is remote. During fiscal 2006 and fiscal 2005, the Company recognized $33 million and $52 million, respectively, of gift card breakage income. Fiscal

2005 was the first year in which the Company recognized gift card breakage income, and therefore, the amount recognized includes the gift card breakage income related to gift cards sold since the inception of the gift card program. This income is recorded as other income and is included in the accompanying Consolidated Statements of Earnings as a reduction in Selling, General and Administrative Expenses ("SG&A").

Services Revenue

Net Sales include services revenue generated through a variety of installation, home maintenance and professional service programs. In these programs, the customer selects and purchases material for a project and the Company provides or arranges professional installation. These programs are offered through the Company's stores and certain HD Supply locations. Under certain programs, when the Company provides or arranges the installation of a project and the subcontractor provides material as part of the installation, both the material and labor are included in services revenue. The Company recognizes this revenue when the service for the customer is complete.

All payments received prior to the completion of services are recorded in Deferred Revenue in the accompanying Consolidated Balance Sheets. Retail services revenue was $3.8 billion, $3.5 billion and $3.0 billion for fiscal 2006, 2005 and 2004, respectively.

Self-Insurance

The Company is self-insured for certain losses related to general liability, product liability, automobile, workers' compensation and medical claims. The expected ultimate cost for claims incurred as of the balance sheet date is not discounted and is recognized as a liability. The expected ultimate cost of claims is estimated based upon analysis of historical data and actuarial estimates.

Prepaid Advertising

Television and radio advertising production costs along with media placement costs are expensed when the advertisement first appears. Included in Other Current Assets in the accompanying Consolidated Balance Sheets are $44 million and $42 million, respectively, at the end of fiscal 2006 and 2005 relating to prepayments of production costs for print and broadcast advertising.

Vendor Allowances

Vendor allowances primarily consist of volume rebates that are earned as a result of attaining certain purchase levels and advertising co-op allowances for the promotion of vendors' products that are typically based on guaranteed minimum amounts with additional amounts being earned for attaining certain purchase levels. These vendor allowances are accrued as earned, with those allowances received as a result of attaining certain purchase levels accrued over the incentive period based on estimates of purchases.

Volume rebates and advertising co-op allowances earned are initially recorded as a reduction in Merchandise Inventories and a subsequent reduction in Cost of Sales when the related product is sold. Certain advertising co-op allowances that are reimbursements of specific, incremental and identifiable costs incurred to promote vendors' products are recorded as an offset against advertising expense. In fiscal 2006, 2005 and 2004, net advertising expense was $1.1 billion, $1.1 billion and $1.0 billion, respectively, which was recorded in SG&A.

Cost of Sales

Cost of Sales includes the actual cost of merchandise sold and services performed, the cost of transportation of merchandise from vendors to the Company's stores, locations or customers, the operating cost of the Company's distribution centers and the cost of deferred interest programs offered through the Company's private label credit card program.

The cost of handling and shipping merchandise from the Company's stores, locations or distribution centers to the customer is classified as SG&A. The cost of shipping and handling, including internal costs and payments to third parties, classified as SG&A was $741 million, $563 million and $499 million in fiscal 2006, 2005 and 2004, respectively.

Goodwill and Other Intangible Assets

Goodwill represents the excess of purchase price over the fair value of net assets acquired. The Company does not amortize goodwill, but does assess the recoverability of goodwill in the third quarter of each fiscal year by determining whether the fair value of each reporting unit supports its carrying value. The fair values of the Company's identified reporting units were estimated using the expected present value of discounted cash flows.

The Company amortizes the cost of other intangible assets over their estimated useful lives, which range from 1 to 14 years, unless such lives are deemed indefinite. Intangible assets with indefinite lives are tested in the third quarter of each fiscal year for impairment. The Company recorded no impairment charges for fiscal 2006, 2005 or 2004.

Impairment of Long-Lived Assets

The Company evaluates the carrying value of long-lived assets when management makes the decision to relocate or close a store or other location, or when circumstances indicate the carrying amount of an asset may not be recoverable. Losses related to the impairment of long-lived assets are recognized to the extent the sum of undiscounted estimated future cash flows expected to result from the use of the asset are less than the asset's carrying value. If the carrying value is greater than the future cash flows, a provision is made to write down the related assets to the estimated net recoverable value. Impairment losses were recorded as a component of SG&A in the accompanying Consolidated Statements of Earnings. When a location closes, the Company also recognizes in SG&A the net present value of future lease obligations, less estimated sublease income.

In fiscal 2005, the Company recorded $91 million in SG&A related to asset impairment charges and on-going lease obligations associated with the closing of 20 of its EXPO stores. Additionally, the Company recorded $29 million of expense in Cost of Sales in fiscal 2005 related to inventory markdowns in these stores. The Company also recorded impairments on other closings and relocations in the ordinary course of business, which were not material to the Consolidated Financial Statements of the Company in fiscal 2006, 2005 and 2004.

Stock-Based Compensation

Effective February 3, 2003, the Company adopted the fair value method of recording stock-based compensation expense in accordance with Statement of Financial Accounting Standards ("SFAS") No. 123, "Accounting for Stock-Based Compensation" ("SFAS 123"). The Company selected the prospective method of adoption as described in SFAS No. 148, "Accounting for Stock-Based Compensation – Transition and Disclosure," and accordingly, stock-based compensation expense was recognized for stock options granted, modified or settled and expense related to the Employee Stock Purchase Plan ("ESPP") after the beginning of fiscal 2003. Effective January 30, 2006, the Company adopted the fair value recognition provisions of SFAS No. 123(R), "Share-Based Payment" ("SFAS 123(R)"), using the modified prospective transition method. Under the modified prospective transition method, the Company began expensing unvested options granted prior to fiscal 2003 in addition to continuing to recognize stock-based compensation expense for all share-based payments awarded since the adoption of SFAS 123 in fiscal 2003. During fiscal 2006, the Company recognized additional stock compensation expense of approximately $40 million as a result of the adoption of SFAS 123(R). As the majority of stock options granted prior to 2003 are now fully vested, the Company does not expect SFAS 123(R) to have a material impact on its consolidated financial condition or results of operations subsequent to fiscal 2006. Results of prior periods have not been restated.

The per share weighted average fair value of stock options granted during fiscal 2006, 2005 and 2004 was $11.88, $12.83 and $13.57, respectively. The fair value of these options was determined at the date of grant using the Black-Scholes option-pricing model with the following assumptions:

	Fiscal Year Ended		
	January 28, 2007	January 29, 2006	January 30, 2005
Risk-free interest rate	4.7%	4.3%	2.6%
Assumed volatility	28.5%	33.7%	41.3%
Assumed dividend yield	1.5%	1.1%	0.8%
Assumed lives of option	5 years	5 years	5 years

The following table illustrates the effect on Net Earnings and Earnings per Share as if the Company had applied the fair value recognition provisions of SFAS 123(R) to all stock-based compensation in each period (amounts in millions, except per share data):

	Fiscal Year Ended		
	January 28, 2007	January 29, 2006	January 30, 2005
Net Earnings, as reported	$5,761	$5,838	$5,001
Add: Stock-based compensation expense included in reported Net Earnings, net of related tax effects	186	110	79
Deduct: Total stock-based compensation expense determined under fair value based method for all awards, net of related tax effects	(186)	(197)	(237)
Pro forma net earnings	$5,761	$5,751	$4,843
Earnings per Share:			
Basic – as reported	$ 2.80	$ 2.73	$ 2.27
Basic – pro forma	$ 2.80	$ 2.69	$ 2.19
Diluted – as reported	$ 2.79	$ 2.72	$ 2.26
Diluted – pro forma	$ 2.79	$ 2.68	$ 2.19

Derivatives

The Company uses derivative financial instruments from time to time in the management of its interest rate exposure on long-term debt. The Company accounts for its derivative financial instruments in accordance with SFAS No. 133, "Accounting for Derivative Instruments and Hedging Activities." There were no derivative instruments outstanding as of January 28, 2007.

Comprehensive Income

Comprehensive Income includes Net Earnings adjusted for certain revenues, expenses, gains and losses that are excluded from Net Earnings under generally accepted accounting principles. Adjustments to Net Earnings are primarily for foreign currency translation adjustments and interest rate hedges.

Foreign Currency Translation

Assets and Liabilities denominated in a foreign currency are translated into U.S. dollars at the current rate of exchange on the last day of the reporting period. Revenues and Expenses are generally translated at a daily exchange rate and equity transactions are translated using the actual rate on the day of the transaction.

Reclassifications

Certain amounts in prior fiscal years have been reclassified to conform with the presentation adopted in the current fiscal year.

2.   STAFF ACCOUNTING BULLETIN NO. 108

In September 2006, the Securities and Exchange Commission ("SEC") issued Staff Accounting Bulletin No. 108, "Considering the Effects of Prior Year Misstatements when Quantifying Misstatements in Current Year Financial Statements" ("SAB 108"). SAB 108 addresses the process of quantifying prior year financial statement misstatements and their impact on current year financial statements. The provisions of SAB 108 allow companies to report the cumulative effect of correcting immaterial prior year misstatements, based on the Company's historical method for evaluating misstatements, by adjusting the opening balance of retained earnings in the current year financial statements rather than amending previously filed reports. SAB 108 is effective for fiscal years ending after November 15, 2006, and therefore was effective for The Home Depot in fiscal 2006. In accordance with SAB 108, the Company has adjusted beginning Retained Earnings for fiscal 2006 in the accompanying Consolidated Financial Statements for the items described below. The Company does not consider these adjustments to have a material impact on the Company's consolidated financial statements in any of the prior years affected.

Historical Stock Option Practices

During fiscal 2006, the Company requested that its Board of Directors review its historical stock option granting practices. A subcommittee of the Audit Committee undertook the review with the assistance of independent outside counsel, and it has completed its review. The principal findings of the review are as follows:

- All options granted in the period from 2002 through the present had an exercise price based on the market price of the Company's stock on the date the grant was approved by the Board of Directors or an officer acting pursuant to delegated authority. During this period, the stock administration department corrected administrative errors retroactively and without separate approvals. The administrative errors included inadvertent omissions of grantees from lists that were approved previously and miscalculations of the number of options granted to particular employees on approved lists.

- All options granted from December 1, 2000 through the end of 2001 had an exercise price based on the market price of the Company's stock on the date of a meeting of the Board of Directors or some other date selected without the benefit of hindsight. The February 2001 annual grant was not finally allocated to recipients until several weeks after the grant was approved. During this period, the stock administration department also corrected administrative errors retroactively and without separate approvals as in the period 2002 to the present.

- For annual option grants and certain quarterly option grants from 1981 through November 2000, the stated grant date was routinely earlier than the actual date on which the grants were approved by a committee of the Board of Directors. In almost every instance, the stock price on the apparent approval date was higher than the price on the stated grant date. The backdating occurred for grants at all levels of the Company. Management personnel, who have since left the Company, generally followed a practice of reviewing closing prices for a prior period and selecting a date with a low stock price to increase the value of the options to employees on lists of grantees subsequently approved by a committee of the Board of Directors.

- The annual option grants in 1994 through 2000, as well as many quarterly grants during this period, were not finally allocated among the recipients until several weeks after the stated grant date. Because of the absence of records prior to 1994, it is unclear whether allocations also postdated the selected grant dates from 1981 through 1993. Moreover, for many of these annual and quarterly grants from 1981 through December 2000, there is insufficient documentation to determine with certainty when the grants were actually authorized by a committee of the Board of Directors. Finally, the Company's stock administration department also retroactively added employees to lists of approved grantees, or changed the number of options granted to specific employees, without authorization of the Board of Directors or a board committee, to correct administrative errors.

- Numerous option grants to rank-and-file employees were made pursuant to delegations of authority that may not have been effective under Delaware law.

- In numerous instances, and primarily prior to 2003, beneficiaries of grants who were required to report them to the SEC failed to do so in a timely manner or at all.

- The subcommittee concluded that there was no intentional wrongdoing by any current member of the Company's management team or its Board of Directors.

The Company believes that because of these errors, it had unrecorded expense over the affected period (1981 through 2005) of $227 million in the aggregate, including related tax items. In accordance with the provisions of SAB 108, the Company decreased beginning Retained Earnings for fiscal 2006 by $227 million within the accompanying Consolidated Financial Statements.

As previously disclosed, the staff of the SEC has begun an informal inquiry into the Company's stock option practices, and the U.S. Attorney for the Southern District of New York has also requested information on the subject. The Company is continuing to cooperate with these agencies. While the Company cannot predict the outcome of these matters, it does not believe that they will have a material adverse impact on its consolidated financial condition or results of operations.

The Company does not believe that the effect of the stock option adjustment was material, either quantitatively or qualitatively, in any of the years covered by the review of these items. In reaching that determination, the following quantitative measures were considered (dollars in millions):

Fiscal Year	Net After-tax Effect of Adjustment	Reported Net Earnings	Percent of Reported Net Earnings
2005	$ 11	$ 5,838	0.19%
2004	18	5,001	0.36
2003	18	4,304	0.42
2002	21	3,664	0.57
1981-2001	159	14,531	1.09
Total	$227	$33,338	0.68%

Vendor Credits

The Company records credits against vendor invoices for various issues related to the receipt of goods. The Company previously identified that it was not recording an allowance for subsequent reversals of these credits based on historical experience. Beginning Retained Earnings for fiscal 2006 has been decreased by $30 million in the accompanying Consolidated Financial Statements to reflect the appropriate adjustments to Merchandise Inventories and Accounts Payable, net of tax.

Impact of Adjustments

The impact of each of the items noted above, net of tax, on fiscal 2006 beginning balances are presented below (amounts in millions):

	Cumulative Effect as of January 30, 2006		
	Stock Option Practices	Vendor Credits	Total
Merchandise Inventories	$ —	$ 9	$ 9
Accounts Payable	—	(59)	(59)
Deferred Income Taxes	11	20	31
Other Accrued Expenses	(37)	—	(37)
Paid-In Capital	(201)	—	(201)
Retained Earnings	227	30	257
Total	$ —	$ —	$ —

3. INTANGIBLE ASSETS

The Company's intangible assets at the end of fiscal 2006 and fiscal 2005, which are included in Other Assets in the accompanying Consolidated Balance Sheets, consisted of the following (amounts in millions):

	January 28, 2007	January 29, 2006
Customer relationships	$ 756	$283
Trademarks and franchises	106	92
Other	67	58
Less accumulated amortization	(151)	(35)
Total	$ 778	$398

Amortization expense related to intangible assets was $117 million, $29 million and $4 million for fiscal 2006, 2005 and 2004, respectively. Estimated future amortization expense for intangible assets recorded as of January 28, 2007 is $107 million, $105 million, $99 million, $94 million and $82 million for fiscal 2007 through fiscal 2011, respectively.

4. DEBT

The Company has a commercial paper program that allows for borrowings up to $2.5 billion. All of the Company's short-term borrowings in fiscal 2006 and 2005 were made under this commercial paper program. In connection with the commercial paper program, the Company has a back-up credit facility with a consortium of banks for borrowings up to $2.0 billion. The credit facility, which expires in December 2010, contains various restrictions, none of which is expected to materially impact the Company's liquidity or capital resources.

Short-Term Debt under the commercial paper program was as follows (dollars in millions):

	January 28, 2007	January 29, 2006
Balance outstanding at fiscal year-end	$ —	$900
Maximum amount outstanding at any month-end	$1,470	$900
Average daily short-term borrowings	$ 300	$ 22
Weighted average interest rate	5.1%	4.3%

The Company's Long-Term Debt at the end of fiscal 2006 and fiscal 2005 consisted of the following (amounts in millions):

	January 28, 2007	January 29, 2006
5.375% Senior Notes; due April 1, 2006; interest payable semi-annually on April 1 and October 1	$ —	$ 500
3.75% Senior Notes; due September 15, 2009; interest payable semi-annually on March 15 and September 15	997	996
Floating Rate Senior Notes; due December 16, 2009; interest payable on March 16, June 16, September 16 and December 16	750	—
4.625% Senior Notes; due August 15, 2010; interest payable semi-annually on February 15 and August 15	997	996
5.20% Senior Notes; due March 1, 2011; interest payable semi-annually on March 1 and September 1	1,000	—
5.25% Senior Notes; due December 16, 2013; interest payable semi-annually on June 16 and December 16	1,243	—
5.40% Senior Notes; due March 1, 2016; interest payable semi-annually on March 1 and September 1	2,986	—
5.875% Senior Notes; due December 16, 2036; interest payable semi-annually on June 16 and December 16	2,958	—
Capital Lease Obligations; payable in varying installments through January 31, 2055	419	381
Other	311	312
Total Long-Term Debt	11,661	3,185
Less current installments	18	513
Long-Term Debt, excluding current installments	$11,643	$2,672

In December 2006, the Company issued $750 million of floating rate Senior Notes due December 16, 2009 at par value, $1.25 billion of 5.25% Senior Notes due December 16, 2013 at a discount of $7 million and $3.0 billion of 5.875% Senior Notes due December 16, 2036 at a discount of $42 million, together the "December 2006 Issuance." The net proceeds of the December 2006 Issuance were used to fund, in part, the Company's common stock repurchases, to repay outstanding commercial paper and for general corporate purposes. The $49 million discount and $37 million of issuance costs associated with the December 2006 Issuance are being amortized to interest expense over the term of the related Senior Notes.

Additionally in October 2006, the Company entered into a forward starting interest rate swap agreement with a notional amount of $1.0 billion, accounted for as a cash flow hedge, to hedge interest rate fluctuations in anticipation of the issuance of the 5.875% Senior Notes due December 16, 2036. Upon issuance of the hedged debt in December 2006, the Company settled its forward starting interest rate swap agreements and recorded an $11 million decrease, net of income taxes, to Accumulated

Other Comprehensive Income, which will be amortized to interest expense over the life of the related debt.

In March 2006, the Company issued $1.0 billion of 5.20% Senior Notes due March 1, 2011 at a discount of $1 million and $3.0 billion of 5.40% Senior Notes due March 1, 2016 at a discount of $15 million, together the "March 2006 Issuance." The net proceeds of the March 2006 Issuance were used to pay for the acquisition price of Hughes Supply, Inc. and for the repayment of the Company's 5.375% Senior Notes due April 2006 in the aggregate principal amount of $500 million. The $16 million discount and $19 million of issuance costs associated with the March 2006 Issuance are being amortized to interest expense over the term of the related Senior Notes.

Additionally in March 2006, the Company entered into a forward starting interest rate swap agreement with a notional amount of $2.0 billion, accounted for as a cash flow hedge, to hedge interest rate fluctuations in anticipation of the issuance of the 5.40% Senior Notes due March 1, 2016. Upon issuance of the hedged debt, the Company settled its forward starting interest rate swap agreements and recorded a $12 million decrease, net of income taxes, to Accumulated Other Comprehensive Income, which will be amortized to interest expense over the life of the related debt.

In August 2005, the Company issued $1.0 billion of 4.625% Notes due August 15, 2010 ("August 2005 Issuance") at a discount of $5 million. The net proceeds of $995 million were used to pay for a portion of the acquisition price of National Waterworks, Inc. The $5 million discount and $7 million of issuance costs associated with the August 2005 Issuance are being amortized to interest expense over the term of the related Senior Notes.

The Company also had $1.0 billion of 3.75% Senior Notes due September 15, 2009 outstanding as of January 28, 2007, collectively referred to with the December 2006 Issuance, March 2006 Issuance and August 2005 Issuance as "Senior Notes." The Senior Notes may be redeemed by the Company at any time, in whole or in part, at a redemption price plus accrued interest up to the redemption date. The redemption price is equal to the greater of (1) 100% of the principal amount of the Senior Notes to be redeemed, or (2) the sum of the present values of the remaining scheduled payments of principal and interest to maturity. Additionally, if a Change in Control Triggering Event occurs, as defined by the terms of the December 2006 Issuance, holders of the December 2006 Issuance have the right to require the Company to redeem those notes at 101% of the aggregate principal amount of the notes plus accrued interest up to the redemption date.

The Company is generally not limited under the indenture governing the Senior Notes in its ability to incur additional indebtedness or required to maintain financial ratios or specified levels of net worth or liquidity. However, the indenture governing the Senior Notes contains various restrictive covenants, none of which is expected to impact the Company's liquidity or capital resources.

Interest Expense in the accompanying Consolidated Statements of Earnings is net of interest capitalized of $47 million, $51 million and $40 million in fiscal 2006, 2005 and 2004, respectively. Maturities of Long-Term Debt are $18 million for fiscal 2007, $301 million for fiscal 2008, $1.8 billion for fiscal 2009, $1.0 billion for fiscal 2010, $1.0 billion for fiscal 2011 and $7.5 billion thereafter.

As of January 28, 2007, the market value of the Senior Notes was approximately $10.9 billion. The estimated fair value of all other long-term borrowings, excluding capital lease obligations, was approximately $316 million compared to the carrying value of $311 million. These fair values were estimated using a discounted cash flow analysis based on the Company's incremental borrowing rate for similar liabilities.

5. INCOME TAXES

The components of Earnings before Provision for Income Taxes for fiscal 2006, 2005 and 2004 were as follows (amounts in millions):

	Fiscal Year Ended		
	January 28, 2007	January 29, 2006	January 30, 2005
United States	$8,709	$8,736	$7,508
Foreign	599	546	404
Total	$9,308	$9,282	$7,912

The Provision for Income Taxes consisted of the following (amounts in millions):

	Fiscal Year Ended		
	January 28, 2007	January 29, 2006	January 30, 2005
Current:			
Federal	$2,831	$3,394	$2,153
State	409	507	279
Foreign	329	156	139
	3,569	4,057	2,571
Deferred:			
Federal	(9)	(527)	304
State	(9)	(111)	52
Foreign	(4)	25	(16)
	(22)	(613)	340
Total	$3,547	$3,444	$2,911

The Company's combined federal, state and foreign effective tax rates for fiscal 2006, 2005 and 2004, net of offsets generated by federal, state and foreign tax benefits, were approximately 38.1%, 37.1% and 36.8%, respectively.

The reconciliation of the Provision for Income Taxes at the federal statutory rate of 35% to the actual tax expense for the applicable fiscal years was as follows (amounts in millions):

	Fiscal Year Ended		
	January 28, 2007	January 29, 2006	January 30, 2005
Income taxes at federal statutory rate	$3,258	$3,249	$2,769
State income taxes, net of federal income tax benefit	261	279	215
Foreign rate differences	5	(10)	(17)
Change in valuation allowance	—	(23)	(31)
Other, net	23	(51)	(25)
Total	$3,547	$3,444	$2,911

The tax effects of temporary differences that give rise to significant portions of the deferred tax assets and deferred tax liabilities as of January 28, 2007 and January 29, 2006, were as follows (amounts in millions):

	January 28, 2007	January 29, 2006
Current:		
Deferred Tax Assets:		
Accrued self-insurance liabilities	$ 94	$ 143
Other accrued liabilities	603	278
Other	—	28
Current Deferred Tax Assets	697	449
Deferred Tax Liabilities:		
Accelerated inventory deduction	(137)	(271)
Other	(29)	(17)
Current Deferred Tax Liabilities	(166)	(288)
Current Deferred Tax Assets, net	531	161
Noncurrent:		
Deferred Tax Assets:		
Accrued self-insurance liabilities	325	354
Other accrued liabilities	—	35
Net operating losses	66	63
Noncurrent Deferred Tax Assets	391	452
Deferred Tax Liabilities:		
Property and equipment	(1,365)	(1,160)
Goodwill and other intangibles	(361)	(209)
Other	(74)	—
Noncurrent Deferred Tax Liabilities	(1,800)	(1,369)
Noncurrent Deferred Tax Liabilities, net	(1,409)	(917)
Net Deferred Tax Liabilities	$ (878)	$ (756)

Current deferred tax assets and current deferred tax liabilities are netted by tax jurisdiction and noncurrent deferred tax assets and noncurrent deferred tax liabilities are netted by tax jurisdiction, and are included in the accompanying Consolidated Balance Sheets as follows (amounts in millions):

	January 28, 2007	January 29, 2006
Other Current Assets	$ 561	$ 221
Other Assets	7	29
Other Accrued Expenses	(30)	(60)
Deferred Income Taxes	(1,416)	(946)
Net Deferred Tax Liabilities	$ (878)	$(756)

The Company believes that the realization of the deferred tax assets is more likely than not, based upon the expectation that it will generate the necessary taxable income in future periods and, accordingly, no valuation reserves have been provided. As a result of acquisitions that were accounted for under the purchase method of accounting, deferred tax liabilities of $118 million were recorded in fiscal 2006 representing the difference between the book value and the tax basis of acquired assets.

50

At January 28, 2007, the Company had state and foreign net operating loss carry-forwards to reduce future taxable income, which will expire at various dates from 2010 to 2026. Management has concluded that it is more likely than not that these tax benefits related to the net operating losses will be realized and hence no valuation allowance has been provided. The Company has not provided for U.S. deferred income taxes on $1.2 billion of undistributed earnings of international subsidiaries because of its intention to indefinitely reinvest these earnings outside the U.S. The determination of the amount of the unrecognized deferred U.S. income tax liability related to the undistributed earnings is not practicable; however, unrecognized foreign income tax credits would be available to reduce a portion of this liability.

The Company's income tax returns are routinely under audit by domestic and foreign tax authorities. These audits include questions regarding its tax filing positions, including the timing and amount of deductions and the allocation of income among various tax jurisdictions. In 2005, the IRS completed its examination of the Company's U.S. federal income tax returns through fiscal 2002. Certain issues relating to the examinations of fiscal 2001 and 2002 are under appeal, the outcome of which is not expected to have a material impact on the Company's financial statements. During 2006, the IRS initiated an audit of the Company's fiscal 2003 and 2004 income tax returns. This audit will likely not be completely settled until after fiscal 2007. At this time, the Company does not expect the results of the audit to have a material impact on the Company's financial statements.

During the second quarter of fiscal 2006, the Quebec National Assembly passed legislation that retroactively changed certain tax laws that subjected the Company to additional tax and interest. As a result, the Company received an assessment from Quebec for $57 million in retroactive tax and $12 million in related interest for the 2002 through 2005 taxable years. This retroactive tax is included in the Company's current year foreign tax expense.

In July 2006, the Financial Accounting Standards Board ("FASB") issued FASB Interpretation No. 48, "Accounting for Uncertainty in Income Taxes – an Interpretation of FASB Statement No. 109" ("FIN 48"). FIN 48 clarifies the accounting for uncertainty in income tax reporting by prescribing a recognition threshold and measurement attribute for the financial statement recognition and measurement of a tax position taken or expected to be taken in a tax return. FIN 48 requires that companies recognize tax benefits in their financial statements for a tax position only if that position is more likely than not of being sustained on audit, based on the technical merits of the position. Additionally, FIN 48 provides guidance on de-recognition, classification, interest and penalties, accounting in interim periods, disclosure and transition. FIN 48 becomes effective for fiscal years beginning after December 15, 2006, and will therefore be effective for The Home Depot in fiscal 2007. The cumulative impact of adopting FIN 48 in fiscal 2007 is not expected to have a material impact on the financial condition of the Company.

6. EMPLOYEE STOCK PLANS

The Home Depot, Inc. 2005 Omnibus Stock Incentive Plan ("2005 Plan") and The Home Depot, Inc. 1997 Omnibus Stock Incentive Plan ("1997 Plan") (collectively the "Plans") provide that incentive, non-qualified stock options, stock appreciation rights, restricted shares, performance shares, performance units and deferred shares may be issued to selected associates, officers and directors of the Company. Under the 2005 Plan, the maximum number of shares of the Company's common stock authorized for issuance is 255 million shares, with any award other than a stock option reducing the number of shares available for issuance by 2.11 shares. As of January 28, 2007, there were 236 million shares available for future grant under the 2005 Plan. No additional equity awards may be issued from the 1997 Plan after the adoption of the 2005 Plan on May 26, 2005.

Under the Plans, as of January 28, 2007, the Company had granted incentive and non-qualified stock options for 184 million shares, net of cancellations (of which 120 million have been exercised). Under the terms of the Plans, incentive stock options and non-qualified stock options are to be priced at or above the fair market value of the Company's stock on the date of the grant. Typically, incentive stock options and non-qualified stock options vest at the rate of 25% per year commencing on the first anniversary date of the grant and expire on the tenth anniversary date of the grant. The Company recognized $148 million, $117 million and $71 million of stock-based compensation expense in fiscal 2006, 2005 and 2004, respectively, related to stock options.

Under the Plans, as of January 28, 2007, the Company had issued 12 million shares of restricted stock, net of cancellations (the restrictions on 2 million shares have lapsed). Generally, the restrictions on the restricted stock lapse according to one of the following schedules: (1) the restrictions on 100% of the restricted stock lapse at 3, 4 or 5 years, (2) the restrictions on 25% of the restricted stock lapse upon the third and sixth year anniversaries of the date of issuance with the remaining 50% of the restricted stock lapsing upon the associate's attainment of age 62, or (3) the restrictions on 25% of the restricted stock lapse upon the third and sixth year anniversaries of the date of issuance with the remaining 50% of the restricted stock lapsing upon the earlier of the associate's attainment of age 60 or the tenth anniversary date. Additionally, certain awards may become non-forfeitable upon the attainment of age 60, provided the associate has had five years of continuous service. The fair value of the restricted stock is expensed over the period during which the restrictions lapse. The Company recorded stock-based compensation expense related to restricted stock of $95 million, $32 million and $22 million in fiscal 2006, 2005 and 2004, respectively.

In fiscal 2006, 2005 and 2004, there were 417,000, 461,000 and 461,000 deferred shares, respectively, granted under the Plans. Each deferred share entitles the associate to one share of common stock to be received up to five years after the vesting date of the deferred share, subject to certain deferral rights of the associate. The Company recorded stock-based compensation expense related to deferred shares of $37 million, $10 million and $14 million in fiscal 2006, 2005 and 2004, respectively.

As of January 28, 2007, there were 2.5 million non-qualified stock options outstanding under non-qualified stock option plans that are not part of the Plans.

The Company maintains two ESPPs (U.S. and non-U.S. plans). The plan for U.S. associates is a tax-qualified plan under Section 423 of the Internal Revenue Code. The non-U.S. plan is not a Section 423 plan. The ESPPs allow associates to purchase up to 152 million shares of common stock, of which 120 million shares have been purchased from inception of the plans. The purchase price of shares under the ESPPs is equal to 85% of the stock's fair market value on the last day of the purchase period. During fiscal 2006, there were 3 million shares purchased under the ESPPs at an average price of $32.06. Under the outstanding ESPPs as of January 28, 2007, employees have contributed $10 million to purchase shares at 85% of the stock's fair market value on the last day (June 30, 2007) of the purchase period. The Company had 32 million shares available for issuance under the ESPPs at January 28, 2007. The Company recognized $17 million, $16 million and $15 million of stock-based compensation in fiscal 2006, 2005 and 2004, respectively, related to the ESPPs.

In total, the Company recorded stock-based compensation expense, including the expense of stock options, ESPPs, restricted stock and deferred stock units, of $297 million, $175 million and $125 million, in fiscal 2006, 2005 and 2004, respectively.

The following table summarizes stock options outstanding at January 28, 2007, January 29, 2006 and January 30, 2005, and changes during the fiscal years ended on these dates (shares in thousands):

	Number of Shares	Weighted Average Option Price
Outstanding at February 1, 2004	87,779	$35.40
Granted	16,713	36.46
Exercised	(7,825)	25.94
Canceled	(10,273)	38.27
Outstanding at January 30, 2005	86,394	$36.12
Granted	17,721	37.96
Exercised	(11,457)	28.83
Canceled	(8,626)	38.65
Outstanding at January 29, 2006	84,032	$37.24
Granted	257	39.53
Exercised	(10,045)	28.69
Canceled	(8,103)	40.12
Outstanding at January 28, 2007	66,141	$38.20

The total intrinsic value of stock options exercised during fiscal 2006 was $120 million.

As of January 28, 2007, there were approximately 66 million stock options outstanding with a weighted average remaining life of 5.6 years and an intrinsic value of $248 million. As of January 28, 2007, there were approximately 47 million options exercisable with a weighted average option price of $39.20 and an intrinsic value of $162 million. As of January 28, 2007, there were approximately 63 million shares vested or expected to ultimately vest.

The following table summarizes restricted stock outstanding at January 28, 2007 (shares in thousands):

	Number of Shares	Weighted Average Grant Date Fair Value
Outstanding at January 29, 2006	5,308	$35.76
Granted	7,575	41.37
Restrictions lapsed	(1,202)	38.03
Canceled	(1,551)	39.00
Outstanding at January 28, 2007	10,130	$39.20

7. LEASES

The Company leases certain retail locations, office space, warehouse and distribution space, equipment and vehicles. While most of the leases are operating leases, certain locations and equipment are leased under capital leases. As leases expire, it can be expected that, in the normal course of business, certain leases will be renewed or replaced.

Certain lease agreements include escalating rents over the lease terms. The Company expenses rent on a straight-line basis over the life of the lease which commences on the date the Company has the right to control the property. The cumulative expense recognized on a straight-line basis in excess of the cumulative payments is included in Other Accrued Expenses and Other Long-Term Liabilities in the accompanying Consolidated Balance Sheets.

The Company has a lease agreement under which the Company leases certain assets totaling $282 million. This lease was originally created under a structured financing arrangement and involves two special purpose entities. The Company financed a portion of its new stores opened in fiscal years 1997 through 2003 under this lease agreement. Under this agreement, the lessor purchased the properties, paid for the construction costs and subsequently leased the facilities to the Company. The Company records the rental payments under the terms of the operating lease agreements as SG&A in the accompanying Consolidated Statements of Earnings.

The $282 million lease agreement expires in fiscal 2008 with no renewal option. The lease provides for a substantial residual value guarantee limited to 79% of the initial book value of the assets and includes a purchase option at the original cost of each property. During fiscal 2005, the Company committed to exercise its option to purchase the assets under this lease for $282 million at the end of the lease term in fiscal 2008.

In the first quarter of fiscal 2004, the Company adopted the revised version of FASB Interpretation No. 46, "Consolidation of Variable Interest Entities" ("FIN 46"). FIN 46 requires consolidation of a variable interest entity if a company's variable interest absorbs a majority of the entity's expected losses or receives a majority of the entity's expected residual returns, or both.

In accordance with FIN 46, the Company was required to consolidate one of the two aforementioned special purpose entities that, before the effective date of FIN 46, met the requirements for non-consolidation. The second special purpose entity that owns the assets leased by the Company totaling $282 million is not owned by or affiliated with the Company, its management or its officers. Pursuant to FIN 46, the Company was not deemed to have a variable interest, and therefore was not required to consolidate this entity.

FIN 46 requires the Company to measure the assets and liabilities at their carrying amounts, which amounts would have been recorded if FIN 46 had been effective at the inception of the transaction. Accordingly, during the first quarter of fiscal 2004, the Company recorded Long-Term Debt of $282 million and Long-Term Notes Receivable of $282 million on the Consolidated Balance Sheets. The Company continues to record the rental payments under the operating lease agreements as SG&A in the Consolidated Statements of Earnings. The adoption of FIN 46 had no economic impact on the Company.

Total rent expense, net of minor sublease income for fiscal 2006, 2005 and 2004 was $958 million, $782 million and $684 million, respectively. Certain store leases also provide for contingent rent payments based on percentages of sales in excess of specified minimums. Contingent rent expense for fiscal 2006, 2005 and 2004 was approximately $9 million, $9 million and $11 million, respectively. Real estate taxes, insurance, maintenance and operating expenses applicable to the leased property are obligations of the Company under the lease agreements.

The approximate future minimum lease payments under capital and all other leases at January 28, 2007 were as follows (in millions):

Fiscal Year	Capital Leases	Operating Leases
2007	$ 78	$ 917
2008	79	846
2009	78	734
2010	80	647
2011	80	566
Thereafter through 2097	928	5,421
	1,323	$9,131
Less imputed interest	904	
Net present value of capital lease obligations	419	
Less current installments	13	
Long-term capital lease obligations, excluding current installments	$ 406	

Short-term and long-term obligations for capital leases are included in the accompanying Consolidated Balance Sheets in Current Installments of Long-Term Debt and Long-Term Debt, respectively. The assets under capital leases recorded in Property and Equipment, net of amortization, totaled $340 million and $304 million at January 28, 2007 and January 29, 2006, respectively.

8.   EMPLOYEE BENEFIT PLANS

The Company maintains active defined contribution retirement plans for its employees ("the Benefit Plans"). All associates satisfying certain service requirements are eligible to participate in the Benefit Plans. The Company makes cash contributions each payroll period up to specified percentages of associates' contributions as approved by the Board of Directors.

The Company also maintains a restoration plan to provide certain associates deferred compensation that they would have received under the Benefit Plans as a matching contribution if not for the maximum compensation limits under the Internal Revenue Code. The Company funds the restoration plan through contributions made to a grantor trust, which are then used to purchase shares of the Company's common stock in the open market.

The Company's contributions to the Benefit Plans and the restoration plan were $159 million, $132 million and $114 million for fiscal 2006, 2005 and 2004, respectively. At January 28, 2007, the Benefit Plans and the restoration plan held a total of 26 million shares of the Company's common stock in trust for plan participants.

9. BASIC AND DILUTED WEIGHTED AVERAGE COMMON SHARES

The reconciliation of basic to diluted weighted average common shares for fiscal 2006, 2005 and 2004 was as follows (amounts in millions):

	Fiscal Year Ended		
	January 28, 2007	January 29, 2006	January 30, 2005
Weighted average common shares	**2,054**	2,138	2,207
Effect of potentially dilutive securities:			
Stock Plans	**8**	9	9
Diluted weighted average common shares	**2,062**	2,147	2,216

Stock plans include shares granted under the Company's employee stock plans as described in Note 6 to the Consolidated Financial Statements. Options to purchase 45.4 million, 55.1 million and 49.1 million shares of common stock at January 28, 2007, January 29, 2006 and January 30, 2005, respectively, were excluded from the computation of Diluted Earnings per Share because their effect would have been anti-dilutive.

10. COMMITMENTS AND CONTINGENCIES

At January 28, 2007, the Company was contingently liable for approximately $1.2 billion under outstanding letters of credit issued for certain business transactions, including insurance programs, trade and construction contracts. The Company's letters of credit are primarily performance-based and are not based on changes in variable components, a liability or an equity security of the other party.

The Company is involved in litigation arising from the normal course of business and in certain securities and derivative litigation matters. In management's opinion, this litigation is not expected to have a material adverse effect on the Company's consolidated financial condition or results of operations.

11. ACQUISITIONS

The following acquisitions completed by the Company were all accounted for under the purchase method of accounting and, accordingly, their results of operations have been consolidated in the Company's financial statements since the date of acquisition. Pro forma results of operations for fiscal 2006, 2005 and 2004 would not be materially different as a result of these acquisitions and therefore are not presented.

During fiscal 2006, the Company made the following acquisitions under its HD Supply segment:

- Burrus Contractors Supply
- Cox Lumber Company
- CTF Supply
- Edson Electric Supply
- Forest Products Supply
- Grafton Utility Supply
- Heartland Waterworks Supply
- Hughes Supply
- Rice Planter Carpets
- Sioux Pipe
- Texas Contractors Supply
- Western Fasteners

Additionally, during fiscal 2006, the Company acquired Home Decorators Collection, The Home Way and Jubilee Home Solutions under its Retail segment.

The aggregate purchase price for acquisitions in fiscal 2006, 2005 and 2004 was $4.5 billion, $2.6 billion and $729 million, respectively, including $3.5 billion for Hughes Supply in fiscal 2006. The Company recorded Goodwill related to the HD Supply segment of $2.8 billion, $1.8 billion and $391 million for fiscal 2006, 2005 and 2004, respectively, and Goodwill related to the Retail segment of $229 million, $111 million and $163 million for fiscal 2006, 2005 and 2004, respectively, in the accompanying Consolidated Balance Sheets. Of the Goodwill recorded in fiscal 2006, approximately $500 million will be deductible for income taxes.

The following table summarizes the estimated fair values of the assets acquired and liabilities assumed at the dates of acquisition for all acquisitions made during fiscal 2006, and is subject to the final fair value determination of certain assets and liabilities (amounts in millions):

Cash	$ 224
Receivables	948
Inventories	874
Property and Equipment	231
Intangible Assets[1]	547
Goodwill	3,007
Other Assets	187
Total assets acquired	6,018
Current Liabilities	1,321
Other Liabilities	193
Total liabilities assumed	1,514
Net assets acquired	$4,504

(1) *Primarily customer relationships and tradenames which are included in Other Assets in the accompanying Consolidated Balance Sheets and are being amortized over a weighted average useful life of 10 years.*

12. SEGMENT INFORMATION

The Company operates in two reportable business segments: Retail and HD Supply. The Retail segment is principally engaged in the operation of retail stores located in the United States, Canada, Mexico and the Company's recently acquired stores in China. The HD Supply segment distributes products and sells installation services to business-to-business customers, including home builders, professional contractors, municipalities and maintenance professionals. The Company identifies segments based on how management makes operating decisions, assesses performance and allocates resources. The first quarter of fiscal 2006 was the first period in which the Company began to report its results of operations in two segments. This change was a result of the purchase of Hughes Supply, which significantly increased the size of HD Supply and resulted in changes in the Company's internal reporting and management structure.

The Retail segment includes The Home Depot stores, EXPO Design Center stores and other retail formats. The Retail segment also includes our retail services business and our catalog and on-line sales businesses.

The HD Supply segment consists of four major platforms: 1) infrastructure, including waterworks and utilities; 2) construction, including construction supply, lumber and building materials, electrical, plumbing/HVAC and interiors; 3) maintenance, including facilities maintenance and industrial PVF; and 4) repair and remodel.

The Company measures the profit of its segments as Operating Income, which is defined as earnings before net interest expense and provision for income taxes. The amounts under the caption Eliminations/Other in the following tables are unallocated corporate overhead, invested cash and short-term investments and intersegment eliminations. Additionally, Operating Income under Eliminations/Other for the fiscal year ended January 28, 2007 includes $129 million of cost associated with executive severance and separation agreements. The following tables present financial information by segment for the fiscal years ended January 28, 2007, January 29, 2006 and January 30, 2005, respectively (amounts in millions):

| | Fiscal Year Ended January 28, 2007 | | | |
	Retail	HD Supply	Eliminations/ Other	Consolidated
Net Sales	$79,027	$12,070	$(260)	$90,837
Operating Income	$ 9,024	$ 800	$(151)	$ 9,673
Interest, net				(365)
Earnings Before Provision for Income Taxes				$ 9,308
Depreciation and Amortization	$ 1,682	$ 194	$ 10	$ 1,886
Total Assets	$42,094	$10,021	$ 148	$52,263
Capital Expenditures	$ 3,321	$ 221	$ —	$ 3,542
Payments for Businesses Acquired, net	$ 305	$ 3,963	$ —	$ 4,268

| | Fiscal Year Ended January 29, 2006 | | | |
	Retail	HD Supply	Eliminations/ Other	Consolidated
Net Sales	$77,022	$ 4,614	$(125)	$81,511
Operating Income	$ 9,058	$ 319	$ (14)	$ 9,363
Interest, net				(81)
Earnings Before Provision for Income Taxes				$ 9,282
Depreciation and Amortization	$ 1,510	$ 63	$ 6	$ 1,579
Total Assets	$39,827	$ 4,517	$ 61	$44,405
Capital Expenditures	$ 3,777	$ 104	$ —	$ 3,881
Payments for Businesses Acquired, net	$ 190	$ 2,356	$ —	$ 2,546

| | Fiscal Year Ended January 30, 2005 | | | |
	Retail	HD Supply	Eliminations/ Other	Consolidated
Net Sales	$71,101	$ 2,040	$ (47)	$73,094
Operating Income	$ 7,812	$ 122	$ (8)	$ 7,926
Interest, net				(14)
Earnings Before Provision for Income Taxes				$ 7,912
Depreciation and Amortization	$ 1,296	$ 20	$ 3	$ 1,319
Total Assets	$36,902	$ 1,406	$ 712	$39,020
Capital Expenditures	$ 3,905	$ 43	$ —	$ 3,948
Payments for Businesses Acquired, net	$ 202	$ 525	$ —	$ 727

Net Sales for the Company outside of the United States were $6.4 billion, $5.3 billion and $4.2 billion during fiscal 2006, 2005 and 2004, respectively. Long-lived assets outside of the United States totaled $2.5 billion and $2.2 billion as of January 28, 2007 and January 29, 2006, respectively.

13. QUARTERLY FINANCIAL DATA (UNAUDITED)

The following is a summary of the quarterly consolidated results of operations for the fiscal years ended January 28, 2007 and January 29, 2006 (dollars in millions, except per share data):

	Net Sales	Gross Profit	Net Earnings	Basic Earnings per Share	Diluted Earnings per Share
Fiscal Year Ended January 28, 2007:					
First Quarter	$21,461	$ 7,228	$1,484	$0.70	$0.70
Second Quarter	26,026	8,380	1,862	0.90	0.90
Third Quarter	23,085	7,537	1,490	0.73	0.73
Fourth Quarter	20,265	6,638	925	0.46	0.46
Fiscal Year	$90,837	$29,783	$5,761	$2.80	$2.79
Fiscal Year Ended January 29, 2006:					
First Quarter	$18,973	$ 6,355	$1,247	$0.58	$0.57
Second Quarter	22,305	7,409	1,768	0.83	0.82
Third Quarter	20,744	6,963	1,538	0.72	0.72
Fourth Quarter	19,489	6,593	1,285	0.61	0.60
Fiscal Year	$81,511	$27,320	$5,838	$2.73	$2.72

Note: The quarterly data may not sum to fiscal year totals due to rounding.

Item 9. Changes in and Disagreements With Accountants on Accounting and Financial Disclosure.

None.

Item 9A. Controls and Procedures.

Disclosure Controls and Procedures

The Company maintains disclosure controls and procedures that are designed to ensure that information required to be disclosed in the Company's Securities Exchange Act reports is recorded, processed, summarized and reported within the time periods specified in the Securities and Exchange Commission's rules and forms, and that such information is accumulated and communicated to the Company's management, including the Chief Executive Officer and Chief Financial Officer, as appropriate, to allow timely decisions regarding required disclosure.

The Company's Chief Executive Officer and Chief Financial Officer have evaluated the effectiveness of the design and operation of the Company's disclosure controls and procedures (as defined in Rules 13a-15(e) and 15d-15(e) under the Securities Exchange Act) as of the end of the period covered by this report. Based on such evaluation, such officers have concluded that, as of the end of the period covered by this report, the Company's disclosure controls and procedures were effective.

Internal Control Over Financial Reporting

There have not been any changes in the Company's internal control over financial reporting (as such term is defined in Rules 13a-15(e) and 15d-15(e) under the Securities Exchange Act) during the fiscal quarter ended January 28, 2007 that have materially affected, or are reasonably likely to materially affect, the Company's internal control over financial reporting.

Management's Report on Internal Control over Financial Reporting

The information required by this item is incorporated by reference to Item 8. "Financial Statements and Supplementary Data" of this report.

Item 9B. Other Information.

None.

PART III

Item 10. Directors, Executive Officers and Corporate Governance.

Information required by this section, other than information regarding the executive officers of the Company which is set forth in Item 4A. "Executive Officers of the Company" of this report, is incorporated by reference to the sections entitled "Election of Directors and Director Biographies," "Board of Directors Information," "General – Section 16(a) Beneficial Ownership Reporting Compliance" and "Audit Committee Report and Fees Paid to Accounting Firm" in the Company's Proxy Statement for the 2007 Annual Meeting of Shareholders (the "Proxy Statement").

Item 11. Executive Compensation.

The information required by this item is incorporated by reference to the sections entitled "Executive Compensation," "Compensation Discussion & Analysis," "Leadership Development and Compensation Committee" and "Director Compensation" in the Company's Proxy Statement.

Item 12. Security Ownership of Certain Beneficial Owners and Management and Related Stockholder Matters.

The information required by this item is incorporated by reference to the sections entitled "Beneficial Ownership of Common Stock" and "Executive Compensation" in the Company's Proxy Statement.

Item 13. Certain Relationships and Related Transactions, and Director Independence.

The information required by this item is incorporated by reference to the section entitled "Board of Directors Information" and "General – Insider Transactions" in the Company's Proxy Statement.

Item 14. Principal Accounting Fees and Services.

The information required by this item is incorporated by reference to the section entitled "Audit Committee Report and Fees Paid to Accounting Firm" in the Company's Proxy Statement.

PART IV

Item 15. Exhibits, Financial Statement Schedules.

(a)(1) Financial Statements

The following financial statements are set forth in Item 8 hereof:

— Consolidated Statements of Earnings for the fiscal years ended January 28, 2007, January 29, 2006, and January 30, 2005;

— Consolidated Balance Sheets as of January 28, 2007 and January 29, 2006;

— Consolidated Statements of Stockholders' Equity and Comprehensive Income for the fiscal years ended January 28, 2007, January 29, 2006 and January 30, 2005;

— Consolidated Statements of Cash Flows for the fiscal years ended January 28, 2007, January 29, 2006 and January 30, 2005;

— Notes to Consolidated Financial Statements;

— Management's Responsibility for Financial Statements and Management's Report on Internal Control Over Financial Reporting; and

— Reports of Independent Registered Public Accounting Firm.

(2) Financial Statement Schedules

All schedules are omitted as the required information is inapplicable or the information is presented in the consolidated financial statements or related notes.

(3) Exhibits

Exhibits marked with an asterisk (*) are incorporated by reference to exhibits or appendices previously filed with the Securities and Exchange Commission, as indicated by the references in brackets. All other exhibits are filed herewith.

*3.1 Amended and Restated Certificate of Incorporation of The Home Depot, Inc. **[Form 10-Q for the fiscal quarter ended August 4, 2002, Exhibit 3.1]**

*3.2 By-Laws, as amended and restated. **[Form 8-K filed on January 8, 2007, Exhibit 3.1]**

*4.1 Indenture dated as of September 16, 2004 between The Home Depot, Inc. and The Bank of New York. **[Form 8-K filed September 17, 2004, Exhibit 4.1]**

*4.2 Indenture, dated as of May 4, 2005, between The Home Depot, Inc. and The Bank of New York Trust Company, N.A., as Trustee. **[Form S-3 (File No. 333-124699) filed May 6, 2005, Exhibit 4.1]**

*4.3 Form of 3.75% Senior Note due September 15, 2009. **[Form 8-K filed on September 17, 2004, Exhibit 4.2]**

*4.4 Form of 4⅝% Senior Note due August 15, 2010. **[Form 10-K for the fiscal year ended January 29, 2006, Exhibit 4.6]**

*4.5 Form of 5.20% Senior Note due March 1, 2011. **[Form 8-K filed March 23, 2006, Exhibit 4.1]**

*4.6 Form of 5.40% Senior Note due March 1, 2016. **[Form 8-K filed March 23, 2006, Exhibit 4.2]**

*4.7 Form of Floating Rate Senior Note due December 16, 2009. **[Form 8-K filed December 19, 2006, Exhibit 4.1]**

*4.8 Form of 5.250% Senior Note due December 16, 2013. **[Form 8-K filed December 19, 2006, Exhibit 4.2]**

*4.9 Form of 5.875% Senior Note due December 16, 2036. **[Form 8-K filed December 19, 2006, Exhibit 4.3]**

*10.1† The Home Depot, Inc. Amended and Restated Employee Stock Purchase Plan, as amended and restated effective July 1, 2003. **[Form 10-Q for the fiscal quarter ended November 2, 2003, Exhibit 10.1]**

*10.2† Amendment No.1 to The Home Depot, Inc. Amended and Restated Employee Stock Purchase Plan, effective July 1, 2004. **[Form 10-Q for the fiscal quarter ended August 1, 2004, Exhibit 10.2]**

*10.3† The Home Depot, Inc. Non-U.S. Employee Stock Purchase Plan. **[Form 10-K for the fiscal year ended February 2, 2003, Exhibit 10.36]**

*10.4† The Home Depot, Inc. 1997 Omnibus Stock Incentive Plan. **[Form 10-Q for the fiscal quarter ended August 4, 2002, Exhibit 10.1]**

*10.5† Form of Executive Officer Restricted Stock Award Pursuant to The Home Depot, Inc. 1997 Omnibus Stock Incentive Plan. **[Form 10-Q for the fiscal quarter ended October 31, 2004, Exhibit 10.1]**

*10.6† Form of Executive Officer Nonqualified Stock Option Award Pursuant to The Home Depot, Inc. 1997 Omnibus Stock Incentive Plan. **[Form 10-Q for the fiscal quarter ended October 31, 2004, Exhibit 10.2]**

*10.7† Form of Outside Director Nonqualified Stock Option Award Pursuant to The Home Depot, Inc. 1997 Omnibus Stock Incentive Plan. **[Form 10-Q for the fiscal quarter ended October 31, 2004, Exhibit 10.3]**

*10.8† Form of Executive Officer Long-Term Incentive Program Performance Unit Award Pursuant to The Home Depot, Inc. 1997 Omnibus Stock Incentive Plan. **[Form 10-Q for the fiscal quarter ended October 31, 2004, Exhibit 10.4]**

*10.9† The Home Depot, Inc. 2005 Omnibus Stock Incentive Plan. **[Form 8-K filed on May 27, 2005, Exhibit 10.8]**

*10.10† Form of Restricted Stock Award Pursuant to The Home Depot, Inc. 2005 Omnibus Stock Incentive Plan. **[Form 8-K filed on March 27, 2007, Exhibit 10.1]**

*10.11† Form of Deferred Share Award (Non-Employee Director) Pursuant to The Home Depot, Inc. 2005 Omnibus Stock Incentive Plan. **[Form 8-K filed on March 27, 2007, Exhibit 10.2]**

*10.12† Form of Deferred Share Award (U.S. Officers) Pursuant to The Home Depot, Inc. 2005 Omnibus Stock Incentive Plan. **[Form 8-K filed on May 27, 2005, Exhibit 10.3]**

*10.13† Form of Deferred Share Award (Mexico) Pursuant to The Home Depot, Inc. 2005 Omnibus Stock Incentive Plan. **[Form 8-K filed on March 27, 2007, Exhibit 10.3]**

*10.14† Form of Deferred Share Award (Canada) Pursuant to The Home Depot, Inc. 2005 Omnibus Stock Incentive Plan. **[Form 8-K filed on March 27, 2007, Exhibit 10.4]**

*10.15†   Form of Nonqualified Stock Option (Non-Employee Directors) Pursuant to The Home Depot, Inc. 2005 Omnibus Stock Incentive Plan. **[Form 8-K filed on March 27, 2007, Exhibit 10.5]**

*10.16†   Form of Nonqualified Stock Option Pursuant to The Home Depot, Inc. 2005 Omnibus Stock Incentive Plan. **[Form 8-K filed on March 27, 2007, Exhibit 10.6]**

*10.17†   Form of Performance Share Award Pursuant to The Home Depot, Inc. 2005 Omnibus Stock Incentive Plan. **[Form 8-K filed on March 27, 2007, Exhibit 10.7]**

*10.18†   Form of Performance Share Award (Mexico) Pursuant to The Home Depot, Inc. 2005 Omnibus Stock Incentive Plan. **[Form 8-K filed on March 27, 2007, Exhibit 10.8]**

*10.19†   Form of Performance Vested Option Award Pursuant to The Home Depot, Inc. 2005 Omnibus Stock Incentive Plan. **[Form 8-K filed on March 27, 2007, Exhibit 10.9]**

*10.20†   Form of LTIP Performance Unit Award Pursuant to The Home Depot, Inc. 2005 Omnibus Stock Incentive Plan. **[Form 8-K filed on March 27, 2007, Exhibit 10.10]**

*10.21†   The Home Depot FutureBuilder Restoration Plan. **[Form 10-K for the fiscal year ended January 28, 2001, Exhibit 10.10]**

*10.22†   Third Amendment To The Home Depot FutureBuilder Restoration Plan, effective March 1, 2004. **[Form 10- Q for the fiscal quarter ended August 1, 2004, Exhibit 10.1]**

*10.23†   Non-Qualified Stock Option and Deferred Stock Unit Plan and Agreement dated as of December 4, 2000. **[Form 10-K for the fiscal year ended January 28, 2001, Exhibit 10.20]**

*10.24†   The Home Depot FutureBuilder for Puerto Rico. **[Form 10-K for the fiscal year ended February 2, 2003, Exhibit 10.35]**

*10.25†   First Amendment To The Home Depot FutureBuilder for Puerto Rico, effective July 5, 2004. **[Form S-8 (File No. 333-125332) filed May 27, 2005, Exhibit 10.3]**

*10.26†   The Home Depot FutureBuilder, a 401(k) and Stock Ownership Plan, as amended and restated effective July 1, 2004. **[Form 10-Q for the fiscal quarter ended October 31, 2004, Exhibit 10.5]**

*10.27†   The Home Depot Long-Term Incentive Plan. **[Form 10-K for the fiscal year ended February 2, 2003, Exhibit 10.42]**

*10.28†   Senior Officers' Bonus Pool Plan, as amended. **[Appendix A to Proxy Statement for the Annual Meeting of Shareholders held May 26, 1999]**

*10.29†   Executive Officers' Bonus Plan. **[Appendix B to Proxy Statement for the Annual Meeting of Shareholders held May 27, 1998]**

*10.30†   Supplemental Executive Choice Program, effective January 1, 1999. **[Form 10-K for the fiscal year ended February 3, 2002, Exhibit 10.15]**

*10.31†   Home Depot U.S.A., Inc. Deferred Compensation Plan for Officers. **[Form 10-K for the fiscal year ended February 2, 2003, Exhibit 10.38]**

*10.32†   The Home Depot Executive Life Insurance, Death Benefit Only Plan. **[Form 10-K for the fiscal year ended February 2, 2003, Exhibit 10.39]**

*10.33†   The Home Depot Executive Physical Program. **[Form 10-K for the fiscal year ended February 2, 2003, Exhibit 10.40]**

*10.34†   The Home Depot Management Incentive Plan. **[Appendix A to Proxy Statement for the Annual Meeting of Shareholders held on May 30, 2003]**

*10.35†   The Home Depot, Inc. Management Incentive Plan Fiscal Year 2007 Performance Measures. **[Form 8-K filed on March 27, 2007, Exhibit 10.11]**

*10.36†   The Home Depot, Inc. Non-Employee Directors' Deferred Stock Compensation Plan. **[Form 10-K for the fiscal year ended February 2, 2003, Exhibit 10.37]**

10.37†   Separation Agreement Between the Company and Robert Nardelli effective as of January 2, 2007.

10.38†   Deferred Payment Trust dated as of January 12, 2007.

*10.39†   Employment Arrangement between Frank Blake and The Home Depot, Inc., dated January 23, 2007. **[Form 8-K/A filed on January 24, 2007, Exhibit 10.1]**

*10.40†   Employment Arrangement between Carol B. Tomé and The Home Depot, Inc., dated January 22, 2007. **[Form 8-K/A filed on January 24, 2007, Exhibit 10.2]**

*10.41†   Employment Arrangement between Joe DeAngelo and The Home Depot, Inc., dated January 23, 2007. **[Form 8-K/A filed on January 24, 2007, Exhibit 10.3]**

*10.42†   Employment Agreement between Dennis M. Donovan and The Home Depot, Inc. dated March 16, 2001. **[Form S-4 (File No. 333-61548) filed May 24, 2001, Exhibit 10.1]**

*10.43†   Deferred Stock Units Plan and Agreement between Dennis M. Donovan and The Home Depot, Inc. dated as of May 31, 2001. **[Form 10-K for the fiscal year ended February 3, 2002, Exhibit 10.25]**

*10.44†   Promissory Note between Dennis M. Donovan and The Home Depot, Inc. dated June 7, 2001. **[Form 10-K for the fiscal year ended February 3, 2002, Exhibit 10.26]**

*10.45†   Employment Agreement between Frank L. Fernandez and The Home Depot, Inc. dated April 2, 2001. **[Form S-4 (File No. 333-61548) filed May 24, 2001, Exhibit 10.2]**

*10.46†   Deferred Stock Units Plan and Agreement between Frank L. Fernandez and The Home Depot, Inc. dated April 2, 2001. **[Form S-4 (File No. 333-61548) filed May 24, 2001, Exhibit 10.3]**

*10.47†   Promissory Note between Frank L. Fernandez and The Home Depot, Inc. dated June 18, 2001. **[Form 10-K for the fiscal year ended February 3, 2002, Exhibit 10.27]**

*10.48†   Employment Agreement between Robert DeRodes and The Home Depot, Inc., effective as of February 7, 2002. **[Form 10-Q for the fiscal quarter ended November 3, 2002, Exhibit 10.2]**

*10.49†   Separation Agreement & Release by and between The Home Depot, Inc. and John H. Costello, dated September 8, 2005. **[Form 10-Q for the fiscal quarter ended October 30, 2005, Exhibit 10.1]**

*10.50   Participation Agreement dated as of October 22, 1998 among The Home Depot, Inc. as Guarantor; Home Depot U.S.A., Inc. as Lessee; HD Real Estate Funding Corp. II as Facility Lender; Credit Suisse Leasing 92A L.P. as Lessor; The Bank of New York as Indenture Trustee; and Credit Suisse First Boston Corporation and Invemed Associates, Inc. as Initial Purchasers. **[Form 10-K for the fiscal year ended January 31, 1999, Exhibit 10.10.]**

*10.51 Master Modification Agreement dated as of April 20, 1998 among The Home Depot, Inc. as Guarantor; Home Depot U.S.A., Inc., as Lessee and Construction Agent; HD Real Estate Funding Corp., as Facility Lender; Credit Suisse Leasing 92A L.P. as Lessor; the lenders named on the Schedule thereto as Lenders; and Credit Suisse First Boston Corporation as Agent Bank. **[Form 10-K for the fiscal year ended January 31, 1999, Exhibit 10.13]**

12 Statement of Computation of Ratio of Earnings to Fixed Charges.

21 List of Subsidiaries of the Company.

23 Consent of Independent Registered Public Accounting Firm.

31.1 Certification of Chief Executive Officer, pursuant to Rule 13a-14(a) promulgated under the Securities Exchange Act of 1934, as amended.

31.2 Certification of Chief Financial Officer, pursuant to Rule 13a-14(a) promulgated under the Securities Exchange Act of 1934, as amended.

32.1 Certification of Chief Executive Officer, pursuant to 18 U.S.C. Section 1350, as adopted pursuant to Section 906 of the Sarbanes-Oxley Act of 2002.

32.2 Certification of Chief Financial Officer, pursuant to 18 U.S.C. Section 1350, as adopted pursuant to Section 906 of the Sarbanes-Oxley Act of 2002.

---

† Management contract or compensatory plan or arrangement required to be filed as an exhibit to this form pursuant to Item 15(a) of this report.

(This page has been left blank intentionally.)

Pursuant to the requirements of Section 13 or 15(d) of the Securities Exchange Act of 1934, the Registrant has duly caused this report to be signed on its behalf by the undersigned, thereunto duly authorized.

THE HOME DEPOT, INC.
(Registrant)

By: _____/s/ FRANCIS S. BLAKE_____

(Francis S. Blake, Chairman & CEO)

Date: March 23, 2007

Pursuant to the requirements of the Securities Exchange Act of 1934, this report has been signed below by the following persons on behalf of the Registrant and in the capacities and on the dates indicated.

Signature	Title	Date
/s/ FRANCIS S. BLAKE (Francis S. Blake)	Chairman & CEO (Principal Executive Officer)	March 23, 2007
/s/ CAROL B. TOMÉ (Carol B. Tomé)	Chief Financial Officer and Executive Vice President – Corporate Services (Principal Financial Officer and Principal Accounting Officer)	March 23, 2007
/s/ DAVID H. BATCHELDER (David H. Batchelder)	Director	March 23, 2007
/s/ GREGORY D. BRENNEMAN (Gregory D. Brenneman)	Director	March 23, 2007
/s/ JOHN L. CLENDENIN (John L. Clendenin)	Director	March 23, 2007
/s/ CLAUDIO X. GONZÁLEZ (Claudio X. González)	Director	March 23, 2007
/s/ MILLEDGE A. HART, III (Milledge A. Hart, III)	Director	March 23, 2007
/s/ BONNIE G. HILL (Bonnie G. Hill)	Director	March 23, 2007
/s/ LABAN P. JACKSON, JR. (Laban P. Jackson, Jr.)	Director	March 23, 2007
/s/ HELEN JOHNSON-LEIPOLD (Helen Johnson-Leipold)	Director	March 23, 2007
/s/ LAWRENCE R. JOHNSTON (Lawrence R. Johnston)	Director	March 23, 2007
/s/ KENNETH G. LANGONE (Kenneth G. Langone)	Director	March 23, 2007
/s/ ANGELO R. MOZILO (Angelo R. Mozilo)	Director	March 23, 2007

(This page has been left blank intentionally.)

10-Year Summary of Financial and Operating Results
The Home Depot, Inc. and Subsidiaries

amounts in millions, except where noted

	10-Year Compound Annual Growth Rate	2006	2005
STATEMENT OF EARNINGS DATA			
Net sales	16.6%	$ 90,837	$ 81,511
Net sales increase (%)	—	11.4	11.5
Earnings before provision for income taxes	19.7	9,308	9,282
Net earnings	19.9	5,761	5,838
Net earnings increase (%)	—	(1.3)	16.7
Diluted earnings per share ($)[2]	20.5	2.79	2.72
Diluted earnings per share increase (%)	—	2.6	20.4
Diluted weighted average number of common shares	—	2,062	2,147
Gross margin – % of sales	—	32.8	33.5
Total operating expenses – % of sales	—	22.1	22.0
Net interest income (expense) – % of sales	—	(0.4)	(0.1)
Earnings before provision for income taxes – % of sales	—	10.3	11.4
Net earnings – % of sales	—	6.3	7.2
BALANCE SHEET DATA AND FINANCIAL RATIOS			
Total assets	18.8%	$ 52,263	$ 44,405
Working capital	10.5	5,069	2,563
Merchandise inventories	16.8	12,822	11,401
Net property and equipment	17.2	26,605	24,901
Long-term debt	25.0	11,643	2,672
Stockholders' equity	15.4	25,030	26,909
Book value per share ($)	16.5	12.71	12.67
Long-term debt-to-equity (%)	—	46.5	9.9
Total debt-to-equity (%)	—	46.6	15.2
Current ratio	—	1.39:1	1.20:1
Inventory turnover	—	4.7x	4.8x
Return on invested capital (%)	—	20.5	22.4
STATEMENT OF CASH FLOWS DATA			
Depreciation and amortization	23.3%	$ 1,886	$ 1,579
Capital expenditures	11.0	3,542	3,881
Payments for businesses acquired, net	—	4,268	2,546
Cash dividends per share ($)	29.5	0.675	0.400
STORE DATA[3]			
Number of stores	15.4%	2,147	2,042
Square footage at fiscal year-end	15.3	224	215
Increase in square footage (%)	—	4.2	7.0
Average square footage per store (in thousands)	—	105	105
STORE SALES AND OTHER DATA			
Comparable store sales increase (decrease) (%)[3][4][5][6]	—	(2.8)	3.1
Weighted average weekly sales per operating store (in thousands)[3]	(1.0)%	$ 723	$ 763
Weighted average sales per square foot ($)[3][4]	(1.1)	358	377
Number of customer transactions[3]	11.1	1,330	1,330
Average ticket ($)[3]	3.4	58.90	57.98
Number of associates at fiscal year-end	14.0	364,400	344,800

(1) Fiscal year 2001 includes 53 weeks; all other fiscal years reported include 52 weeks.
(2) Diluted earnings per share for fiscal 1997, excluding a $104 million non-recurring charge, were $0.55.
(3) Includes Retail Segment only.
(4) Adjusted to reflect the first 52 weeks of the 53-week fiscal year in 2001.

2004	2003	2002	2001[1]	2000	1999	1998	1997
$ 73,094	$ 64,816	$ 58,247	$ 53,553	$ 45,738	$ 38,434	$ 30,219	$24,156
12.8	11.3	8.8	17.1	19.0	27.2	25.1	23.7
7,912	6,843	5,872	4,957	4,217	3,804	2,654	1,898
5,001	4,304	3,664	3,044	2,581	2,320	1,614	1,160
16.2	17.5	20.4	17.9	11.3	43.7	31.9	23.7
2.26	1.88	1.56	1.29	1.10	1.00	0.71	0.52
20.2	20.5	20.9	17.3	10.0	40.8	29.1	20.9
2,216	2,289	2,344	2,353	2,352	2,342	2,320	2,287
33.4	31.8	31.1	30.2	29.9	29.7	28.5	28.1
22.6	21.2	21.1	20.9	20.7	19.8	19.7	19.8
—	—	0.1	—	—	—	—	—
10.8	10.6	10.1	9.3	9.2	9.9	8.8	7.9
6.8	6.6	6.3	5.7	5.6	6.0	5.3	4.8
$ 39,020	$ 34,437	$ 30,011	$ 26,394	$ 21,385	$ 17,081	$ 13,465	$11,229
3,818	3,774	3,882	3,860	3,392	2,734	2,076	2,004
10,076	9,076	8,338	6,725	6,556	5,489	4,293	3,602
22,726	20,063	17,168	15,375	13,068	10,227	8,160	6,509
2,148	856	1,321	1,250	1,545	750	1,566	1,303
24,158	22,407	19,802	18,082	15,004	12,341	8,740	7,098
11.06	9.93	8.38	7.71	6.46	5.36	3.95	3.23
8.9	3.8	6.7	6.9	10.3	6.1	17.9	18.4
8.9	6.1	6.7	6.9	10.3	6.1	17.9	18.4
1.37:1	1.40:1	1.48:1	1.59:1	1.77:1	1.75:1	1.73:1	1.82:1
4.9x	5.0x	5.3x	5.4x	5.1x	5.4x	5.4x	5.4x
21.5	20.4	18.8	18.3	19.6	22.5	19.3	16.1
$ 1,319	$ 1,076	$ 903	$ 764	$ 601	$ 463	$ 373	$ 283
3,948	3,508	2,749	3,393	3,574	2,618	2,094	1,464
727	215	235	190	26	101	6	61
0.325	0.26	0.21	0.17	0.16	0.11	0.08	0.06
1,890	1,707	1,532	1,333	1,134	930	761	624
201	183	166	146	123	100	81	66
9.8	10.2	14.1	18.5	22.6	23.5	22.8	23.1
106	107	108	109	108	108	107	106
5.1	3.7	(0.5)	—	4	10	7	7
$ 766	$ 763	$ 772	$ 812	$ 864	$ 876	$ 844	$ 829
375	371	370	388	415	423	410	406
1,295	1,246	1,161	1,091	937	797	665	550
54.89	51.15	49.43	48.64	48.65	47.87	45.05	43.63
323,100	298,800	280,900	256,300	227,300	201,400	156,700	124,400

(5) *Includes Net Sales at locations open greater than 12 months, including relocated and remodeled stores. Retail stores become comparable on the Monday following their 365th day of operation. Comparable store sales is intended only as supplemental information and is not a substitute for Net Sales or Net Earnings presented in accordance with generally accepted accounting principles.*

(6) *Comparable store sales in fiscal years prior to 2002 were reported to the nearest percent.*

Corporate and Shareholder Information

STORE SUPPORT CENTER
The Home Depot, Inc.
2455 Paces Ferry Road, NW
Atlanta, GA 30339-4024
Telephone: (770) 433-8211

THE HOME DEPOT WEB SITE
www.homedepot.com

TRANSFER AGENT AND REGISTRAR
Computershare Trust Company, N.A.
P.O. Box 43078
Providence, RI 02940-3078
Telephone: (800) 577-0177
Internet address: www.computershare.com/investor

**INDEPENDENT REGISTERED PUBLIC
ACCOUNTING FIRM**
KPMG LLP
Suite 2000
303 Peachtree Street, NE
Atlanta, GA 30308

STOCK EXCHANGE LISTING
New York Stock Exchange
Trading symbol - HD

ANNUAL MEETING
The Annual Meeting of Shareholders will be held at
9 a.m., Eastern Time, May 24, 2007, at Cobb Galleria
Centre in Atlanta, Georgia.

NUMBER OF SHAREHOLDERS
As of March 26, 2007, there were approximately
180,000 shareholders of record and approximately
1,700,000 individual shareholders holding stock
under nominee security position listings.

DIVIDENDS DECLARED PER COMMON SHARE

	First Quarter	Second Quarter	Third Quarter	Fourth Quarter
Fiscal 2006	**$0.150**	**$0.150**	**$0.225**	**$0.225**
Fiscal 2005	$0.100	$0.100	$0.100	$0.150

**DIRECT STOCK PURCHASE/DIVIDEND
REINVESTMENT PLAN**
New investors may make an initial investment,
and shareholders of record may acquire additional
shares, of our common stock through our direct
stock purchase and dividend reinvestment plan.
Subject to certain requirements, initial cash
investments, cash dividends and/or additional
optional cash purchases may be invested through
this plan.

To obtain enrollment materials, including the
prospectus, access The Home Depot web site,
or call (877) HD-SHARE or (877) 437-4273.
For all other communications regarding these
services, contact Computershare.

**FINANCIAL AND OTHER COMPANY
INFORMATION**
Our Annual Report on Form 10-K for the fiscal year
ended January 28, 2007 is available on our web site
at www.homedepot.com under the Investor Relations
section. In addition, financial reports, filings with the
Securities and Exchange Commission, news releases
and other information are available on The Home
Depot web site.

The Home Depot, Inc. has included as exhibits
to its Annual Report on Form 10-K for the fiscal
year ended January 28, 2007 certifications of
The Home Depot's Chief Executive Officer and
Chief Financial Officer. The Home Depot's
Chief Executive Officer has also submitted to the
New York Stock Exchange (NYSE) a certificate
certifying that he is not aware of any violations
by The Home Depot of the NYSE corporate
governance listing standards.

QUARTERLY STOCK PRICE RANGE

	First Quarter	Second Quarter	Third Quarter	Fourth Quarter
Fiscal 2006				
High	**$43.95**	**$41.61**	**$38.24**	**$41.84**
Low	**$38.50**	**$32.85**	**$33.07**	**$35.77**
Fiscal 2005				
High	$42.99	$43.98	$43.39	$43.27
Low	$34.56	$35.54	$37.14	$39.65

 This paper contains fiber from well-managed,
independently certified forests and contains 10%
post consumer recycled fiber.

Concept and Design: Sagepath (www.sagepath.com)
Photography: Ambrosi, Craig Bromley, Doug Coulter
Printer: Cenveo